GW01460056

DEATH AND MARRIAGE: GREEK AND ROMAN DRAMA

For Anthony Roche

scaenicae artis fautori

DEATH AND MARRIAGE: GREEK AND ROMAN DRAMA

By BRIAN ARKINS

CARYSFORT PRESS

A Carysfort Press Book
Death and Marriage: Greek and Roman Drama
By Brian Arkins
First published in Ireland in 2018 as a paperback original by
Carysfort Press, 58 Woodfield, Scholarstown Road
Dublin 16, Ireland

ISBN 978-0-9955881-0-3

©2017 Copyright remains with the author

Typeset by Carysfort Press
Cover design by eprint limited
Printed and bound by eprint limited
Unit 35
Coolmine Industrial Estate
Dublin 15
Ireland

Caution: All rights reserved. No part of this book may be printed or reproduced or utilized in any form or by any electronic, mechanical, or other means, now known or hereafter invented including photocopying and recording, or in any information storage or retrieval system without permission in writing from the publishers.

This book is sold subject to the conditions that it shall not, by way of trade or otherwise, be lent, resold, hired out, or otherwise circulated in any form of binding, or cover other than that in which it is published and without a similar condition, including this condition, being imposed on the subsequent purchaser.

CONTENTS

1 – BASICS

The Greeks invented, for the West, the dramatic genres of tragedy and comedy. Athens, in the fifth century, was the crucial venue for these plays. They spread to Sicily and to Macedonia.

Tragedies and comedies in Athens were performed at the Spring and Winter festivals of the god Dionysus – a god, basically, of transformation: as in religious ecstasy; in rising again after death; in wine; in the art of the theatre and its masks. Nietzsche posited a famous dichotomy between the irrational Dionysus and the rational Apollo.

Plays in Athens were part of a *civic* occasion. The ten generals poured a libation. Tribute from the subject states was displayed. Orphans, whose fathers died for Athens, were paraded. For all that, comedy and tragedy brought the ideology of the Athenian state into question.

Byron asserts that 'All tragedies are ended by a death,/All comedies are ended by a marriage'. Toxic matter from the past leads to death in tragedy. As Tom Stoppard puts it, 'You're familiar with the tragedies of antiquity, are you? The great homicidal classics?' So Sophocles' *Antigone* concludes with death in the form of three suicides: Antigone, her fiancé Haemon, his mother Eurydice. So Atreus, at the end of Seneca's *Thyestes*, kills his brother's two children.

Aristophanes' *Peace* sees the wedding of Trygaios and Opera. The comedies of Menander typically proceed to the goal of marriage between a young man and young woman. This type of plot is followed in Rome by the comedies of Plautus and Terence.

Tragedy is, for many, a uniquely valuable form of art. Richards sees it as 'perhaps the most general, all-accepting, all-ordering experience known'. Because, argues, Schopenhauer, 'the presentation of a great misfortune is alone essential to tragedy'. But some believe comedy is the more inclusive genre. Patrick Kavanagh held that 'Tragedy is underdeveloped comedy'. Comedy gives the *body* its due in a way that tragedy does not.

Divisions between these two genres are not always clear-cut. Athenian tragedies can have positive endings. The vendetta in the House of Atreus is brought to an end in the *Oresteia* trilogy of Aeschylus. A number of late plays of Euripides – *Orestes*, *Helen*, *Ion*, *Iphigeneia among the Tauri* – have satisfactory endings. In this they are anticipating the comedies of Menander.

A further nuance: tragic dramatists in Athens had to provide not only three tragedies, but also a satyr play (such as the *Cyclops* of Euripides). Satyrs were wild attendants of Dionysus, part animal, much given to lust. These plays clearly offered a comic take on tragic myth. They offered a type of comic relief with an emphasis on pleasure.

The plots of Greek tragedy and Greek comedy are very different. Myth provides the subject matter of all the Athenian tragedies we possess (except for the *Persians* of Aeschylus). Yeats points out that we can *believe* in a myth, but only assent to philosophy. Wallace Stevens sees Greek mythology as 'the greatest piece of fiction'. Historical events, on the other hand, were too close to the bone. When Phrynichus staged his play *The Capture of Miletus* about the annihilation of that city by the Persians in 494, the audience reacted badly. They wept, they fined him 1,000 drachmas.

Myth gave readymade plots to dramatists. But since there is no such thing as a definitive version of a Greek myth, dramatists could adapt these stories for their own purposes. Euripides invents Electra's marriage to a poor farmer in his *Electra*. New in Sophocles' *Antigone* are the condemnation of Antigone and her suicide.

Myth could also function in Athens and in Rome to comment, in an *oblique* way, on contemporary events – a type of distancing effect. Euripides' tragedy *The Trojan Women*, staged in 415, suggested the brutal treatment of the island of Melos by Athens the previous year. Seneca's tragedies about Greek myth suggest the excesses of early Roman Emperors such as Nero.

This distancing process continues in the modern world. As in Anouilh's *Antigone*, staged in Nazi-occupied Paris in 1944. The Nazis could endorse Creon as a collaborator with the Vichy government. The French resistance could endorse Antigone as an opponent of that government.

Comedy's subject matter is very different. Here the dramatist must *invent* plots. Plots about contemporary life, whether these be weighty issues about Athens in Aristophanes, or boy-meets-girl in Menander.

Drama in Athens and in Rome was staged at festivals of the gods; the plays often dealt with religious themes. Dionysus appears in person in Euripides' *Bacchae*. Ritual to appease the gods is found in Aeschylus' *Libation Bearers*, where Clytemnestra offers libations to the murdered Agamemnon. The female festival of the Thesmophoria is the setting for Aristophanes' *Women at the Thesmophoria*. The rite in Seneca's *Oedipus* is unsuccessful, and gods do not feature in his *Phaedra*.

Greek and Roman authors ascribed to literature a *moral* function. In Aristophanes' *The Frogs*, the character 'Aeschylus' claims that 'poets are the teachers of men'. Horace wants literature to be didactic, to be 'useful'. Recently, Shaw wanted his plays to convey a message, and wrote elaborate Prefaces to indicate what it was. These views seem crude. But literature can provide a form of knowledge.

The plays of fifth century Athens were staged in the Theatre of Dionysus on the southern slopes of the Acropolis, which was later renovated under Pericles. The audience for plays was very large: about 15,000 (6,000 attended the political Assembly). Most of the spectators were male citizens, with some resident aliens, and some foreigners. Whether women attended is a hotly debated question.

Plato took a dim view of this large audience, labelling it as *theokratia*, 'sovereignty of the spectators'. Indeed Athens set up the Theoric Fund to enable poor people to attend the theatre. The amount per person was small, 2 obols, half a day's wage. But the ideology is clear: theatre is for all social classes.

Nowadays, despite various types of alternative theatre, the audience is mostly middle class, highly educated, older.

But even in Athens there was some hierarchy. Seats were reserved for members of the Council (Boule), and for priests of Dionysus. There was hierarchy too amid the dramatists. The Greeks believed in competition, in *winning* – in war, in politics, in the law courts, in the Olympic and other games. So in the theatre, both tragic and comic dramatists competed for first prize (a garland of ivy), as did the actors in tragedy.

One thing that made Greek plays attractive was their *brevity*. No sub-plots. Euripides' *Cyclops* comes to just over 700 lines. Three Athenian tragedies could fit into the Second Quarto of *Hamlet*. Then Athenian and Senecan tragedy 'keep to a few families' (Aristotle). For George Steiner, the Western drama we have often deals with the relations 'between gods and men in a small number of Greek households'.

The Chorus is the aspect of Greek and Senecan tragedy most alien to the modern world. In Athens, it was financed and arranged by a wealthy citizen (*choregus*). It numbered 12, later 15, in Greek tragedy, 24 in comedy and possibly 3 in Seneca. Female choruses in extant Greek tragedy outnumber male ones by 21 to 10. But the actors were all male – as in Shakespeare's time.

In comedy, the chorus speak to the audience directly in the *Parabasis*. They speak both in character and as the dramatist's mouthpiece. Less directly, the chorus in tragedy provide collective witness to events and can exhibit an immense range of emotion, including being perplexed.

All Greek and Latin plays were written in verse and thus allowed for elaborate speeches that suit kings, queens, heroes, prophets. But there are speeches too by much less elevated persons. D.H. Lawrence notes that 'When I read Shakespeare I am struck with wonder that such trivial people should muse and thunder in such lovely language.'

The central metre of Greco-Roman drama is iambic trimeter, six iambic feet per line, pattern short/long which was thought closest to ordinary speech. Shakespeare used five iambic feet per line. For Ezra Pound, 'to break the pentameter that was the first heave'. Choral odes in Greco-Roman drama employ a wide variety of lyric metres.

Drama in Rome did not have the kind of civic status it had in fifth century Athens. Elite Romans were forbidden to appear on stage (Nero's acting horrified them); actors were despised. But Rome granted a form of public sanction to drama. State officials organized a substantial season of plays at city festivals. Socially diverse audiences could demand populist types of entertainment: a bear or boxers, says Horace (compare the bear garden near London's Globe).

Latin literature boasts two original genres: love poetry and verse satire. Otherwise, Latin writers appropriate Greek literature to produce something new. Eliot points out that 'mature poets steal ... and make it into something better, or at least something different'. So Plautus and Terence steal from Menander, and Seneca from Greek tragedy.

Key aspects of Euripides. He is a dramatist who disturbs, who is a chameleon, because a dramatic poet must portray all kinds of thoughts: as in the position of women in society (*Medea*); in the morality of war (*The Trojan Women*); s in the validity of ecstatic religion (*The Bacchae*); in the ethics of human sacrifice (*Iphigeneia in Aulis*) – all these plays stressing the experience of women.

Euripides does not do simple. Take *Orestes*. When Orestes kills his mother Clytemnestra and her lover Aegisthus, he is sentenced to death by the citizens of Argos. Helen of Troy appears, and then disappears. Orestes plans to kill Hermione, daughter of Menelaus, unless he helps him. Then the god Apollo (*deus ex machina*) explains all. Helen has gone to heaven. Orestes, freed after his trial in Athens, will marry Hermione, will rule in Argos. This surprise ending is noted by the chorus (whether written by Euripides or not): 'the gods effect many things not expected; /things envisaged are not fulfilled'.

Key aspects of Sophocles. We possess 7 plays by Sophocles out of a total of some 120. Yeats held that 'we might, had the total works of Sophocles survived ... not think him (Shakespeare) greatest'. Matthew Arnold believed that Sophocles 'saw life steadily and saw it whole'. This will never do. In his powerful plays, Sophocles portrays narrow facets of human life – as with intransigent protagonists, male and female, who stick to their principles no matter what; Persons who are against the world (*contra mundum*): Antigone and Electra, Ajax and Philoctetes.

Besides, six suicides in Sophocles cannot be the whole of life. Antigone has 3, plus Jocasta, Ajax, Herakles. Never to be born seems best.

Key aspects of Aeschylus. He is not to be read in the same way as Shakespeare since his magnificent mode is very foreign. There is little stage action, or development of plot, or stress on character. Instead, we find a highly charged atmosphere of looming disaster, presided over by powerful, enigmatic, arbitrary gods.

Only 6 plays of Aeschylus survive (*Prometheus Bound* is not by him). But Nietzsche finds that he co-ordinates speech, song, music, dance – as Euripides does not. Could Aesop's fable of the hedgehog and the fox – made famous by Isaiah Berlin – apply to the Athenian tragedians? The hedgehog knows one big thing: Aeschylus. The fox knows many things: Euripides.

Key aspects of Seneca. He wrote 8 tragedies in early Imperial Rome, but was also a politician and philosopher. Artaud, who championed the Theatre of Cruelty, called Seneca 'the greatest tragic writer in history', because his unique closeness to the excesses and absolute power of Emperors such as Nero required a tragic vision.

Seneca's plays can be staged, as with Ted Hughes' *Oedipus*; as with Caryl Churchill's *Thyestes*. Elizabethan and Jacobean dramatists – not least Shakespeare – knew his worth. Now we do too.

Seneca does shock: thematic shock – when the evil ruler Atreus kills his brother's children and serves them to their father Thyestes in a cannibal meal; verbal shock through the use of hyperbole, paradox, aphorisms.

Key aspects of Aristophanes. His plays are about big issues in fifth century Athens: war, politics, feminism, philosophy, tragedy. The comedies are closer to *satire* than to any type of social comedy. They involve the concept of Utopia that may or may not be realized – realized when in Aristophanes a resourceful hero or heroine remedies an unsatisfactory situation by engineering a triumph of benign fantasy over reality.

Sex in Aristophanes is treated in a very down-to-earth way, with plenty of obscenity and double entendres. What counts is the demands of the body.

Key aspects of Menander, Plautus, Terence. Only one complete play of Menander survives (*The Bad-tempered Man*), together with sizable parts of 9 others, but he became a vital resource for later comic dramatists, starting with Plautus and Terence in Rome.

This type of comedy abandoned *public* themes in order to write of *private* themes, especially that of love. As Ovid wrote, 'Never did delightful Menander write a play without a love interest' (*Tristia* 2.369). It involves love between boy and girl who eventually get married, and it involves other stock characters: 'the running slave,/good married women, bad courtesans,/ a greedy parasite, a boastful soldier, an old man deceived by a slave,/love, hate, suspicion' (Terence, *Eunuchus* 36-39).

Plautus is different from Menander. He is funny. Very. Bakhtin states that 'It was Rome that taught European culture to laugh and ridicule'. Plautus brings to his plays broad Italian humour. A further innovation was to make extensive use of *sung* lyrics (*cantica*).

Terence is refined, low key, quotable. But Julius Caesar, while acknowledging that he was 'a lover of pure language', thought he lacked 'comic force'. An original facet of Terence is to write Prologues that expound his aesthetic doctrines – such as to make use of *two* Greek plays at the same time.

2 – FEMALE INTRUDERS

Johann Gottfried Herder said 'no fact shows more decisively the true character of a man or a nation than their treatment of women'. Athens in the fifth century failed to treat women well. Their very restrictive lives excluded them from politics, war, the law courts, the Olympic and other games. Women played an important *public* part in religion, but their main role was *private*: marriage, producing legitimate children.

And yet. And yet. Women were extremely prominent in Athenian drama of the fifth century: Medea, Antigone, Lysistrata, to go no further. Virginia Woolf explains that this was also a modern phenomenon (1929): if a woman had no existence save in the fiction written by men, one would imagine her a person of the utmost importance. But this woman is in fiction. In fact ... she was locked up, beaten and flung about the room. A very queer, composite being thus emerges. Imaginatively she is of the highest importance; practically she is completely insignificant.

The classicist Helena Foley deals with the same issue in Greece:

> Although women in fact play virtually no public role other than a religious one in the political and social life of ancient Greece, they dominate the imaginative life of Greek men to a degree almost unparalleled in the Western tradition ... Greek writers used the female – in a fashion that bore little relation to the lives of actual women – to understand, express, criticize, and experiment with the problems and contradictions of their culture.

Women in Rome at the time of the Early Empire enjoyed a much freer life. They were educated, attended the symposium, moved easily around Rome. They could divorce men without difficulty, could inherit property. So women in Seneca's tragedies do not appear so radically different from real women. More: certain aristocratic women play an important role behind the scenes in politics. Agrippina ensured that her son Nero became Emperor.

It is certain that what counts in Greek depiction of tragic and comic women is the *imagination of men*. This is seen by Shakespeare in a very emphatic way: (*A Midsummer Night's Dream* 5.1.14-17):

> And, as imagination bodies forth
> The forms of things unknown, the poet's pen
> Turns them to shapes, and gives to airy nothing
> A local habitation and a name.

MEDEA

Euripides and Seneca wrote tragedies about Medea. Dumped by her husband Jason, Medea is intent on revenge. Tony Harrison sees this scenario as archetypal: 'Beneath *all* Greek mythology/are struggles between HE and SHE/ that we're still waging./ In every quiet suburban wife/ is MEDEA, raging.' Euripides does not deal with an eternal triangle in the modern sense. Rather: Jason *loved* Medea, but now wishes to be *married* to the Corinthian princess Glauke. Longing for the *security* of a royal marriage. Medea's revenge does not involve killing Jason: she kills his new wife, that woman's father, and, shockingly, her own two children. 'Heaven hath no rage like love to hatred turned,/ Nor hell a fury like a woman scorned' (Congreve).

Medea laments the inferior status of women in a powerful speech:

> Our greatest struggle is
> To see whether we had a good or
> Bad man. Divorce for women brings ill repute
> And we cannot refuse a husband ...
> They say we live a life without danger
> At home, while they fight in war.
> But they reckon wrongly.
> I would rather stand three times in battle
> Than give birth once.

Childbirth in the Greco-Roman world was hazardous in the extreme.

After her revenge, Medea needs to escape from Corinth. She gets Aegeus, king of Athens, to promise sanctuary. And his being childless alerts Medea to the fact that men are vulnerable about children. So the chariot of the Sungod, her grandfather, carries Medea to Athens. A female figure who cannot be viewed in a purely naturalist way – one to send shivers down male backs in the Theatre of Dionysus in 431 CE.

Seneca's *Medea* opens with the word 'gods' (*di*) from Medea, and closes with the word 'gods' (*deos*) from Jason. Two occurrences that are quite different. Medea calls on the gods of marriage – Juno, Hymenaeus – because Jason has broken his vows. After her murder of their children, Jason asserts that, wherever she goes, there are no gods. Eliot said 'I can think of no play which reserves such a shock for the last word'.

Seneca's *Medea* differs from that of Euripides in several ways:
>Medea is skilled in magic, summons every kind of serpent.
>The chorus is favourable to Jason, not Medea
>Medea sees the ghost of her murdered brother, Apsyrus.
>There is no mention of Aegeus.
>While Euripides' Medea takes her children into exile, Seneca's Medea must leave them behind in Corinth.

Seneca's *Medea* features instances of the meta-theatrical. This happens on four occasions:
>*Medea superest*, Medea remains.
>*Medea fiam*, I will become Medea.
>*Medea nunc sum*, Now I am Medea.
>*Sic fugere soleo*. I usually escape in this way.

This is a device stolen by Elizabethan and Jacobean dramatists, notably by Shakespeare in *Antony and Cleopatra*: 'I am Antony yet', 'I will be Cleopatra'.

ANTIGONE

Sophocles' *Antigone* became, in the twentieth century, a paradigm to explore the clash between a repressive State and the individual person. Between King Creon of Thebes and his niece

Antigone. So much for Matthew Arnold's assertion of 1853 that 'it is no longer possible that we should feel any deep interest in the *Antigone* of Sophocles'.

Background. The two sons of Oedipus, Eteocles (True Glory) and Polyneices (Much Strife) argue about which of them should rule Thebes. Neither does, because they kill each other. Creon, now king, decrees that Polyneices cannot be buried, since he was a traitor who attacked Thebes.

Burial of a dead person, was, for the Greeks, an essential religious rite, which ensured that the person had peace in the afterlife. So Antigone insists on burying her brother Polyneices, edict or no edict. She is the most intransigent of Sophocles' heroic figures. *Antigone* enacts the fifth century debate between the claims of nature (*physis*) on the one hand and custom/law (*nomos*) on the other hand. Antigone is nature, Creon is law. Hegel famously claimed that *both* Creon *and* Antigone are right. This is not the case. The blind prophet Teiresias – always a source of truth in Greek tragedy – makes it crystal clear that Antigone is right, Creon wrong. 'Teiresias makes it clear that Creon has offended against the law of the gods' (Lloyd-Jones).

Antigone concerns the burial of the dead, and in the end Death rules. Antigone hangs herself. Both her fiancé Haemon and his mother Eurydice kill themselves with a sword. Creon is left as a living dead man. Here there is no redemption.

Two plays related in theme to *Antigone* are Aeschylus' *Seven against Thebes* and Euripides' *The Suppliant Women*.

Aeschylus' tragedy (first prize is 467) recounts the attack on Thebes by seven warriors from Argos, which leads to their deaths, including that of Polyneices. Central is the very Greek issue of how the capture of a city (*Polis*) is a disaster.

Euripides' play (423-21) deals with the fact that the Argive warriors are denied burial by Theban rulers. Their mourning mothers arrive near Athens as suppliants asking for burial. The king of Athens, Theseus – a significant figure in the city's prehistory – defeats the Thebans, and ensures the Argive warriors are deeply cremated. The role of women in lamenting the dead is shown to be effective.

PHAEDRA

Euripides produced two versions of *Hippolytus*, the only known redrafting of the same topic by the same Greek dramatist. The second play, the one we have, won first prize in 428. Phaedra is married to the king of Athens, Theseus, and has a stepson Hippolytus. She conceives an illicit sexual passion for her stepson. Stepmothers were distrusted in Greek culture because – as here – they could be involved sexually with a stepchild. In the absence of her husband, Phaedra can indulge her passion for Hippolytus; but she suppresses her feelings – which she does not in the first version.

Phaedra is a devotee of the goddess of sexual love, Aphrodite. Hippolytus is the polar opposite: he utterly rejects sex, worships the goddess Artemis, who represents *separation*: as a virgin, as giving birth, as champion of the wild. When the nurse betrays Phaedra to Hippolytus, disaster follows. Phaedra hangs herself. But she is no innocent: she claims to Theseus that Hippolytus is her seducer. The king makes Hippolytus a scapegoat who must leave the city. Theseus makes the sea god Poseidon send a monstrous bull against him, a symbol of rampant male sexuality. This causes the death of Hippolytus. But first he absolves Theseus of guilt, and there is reconciliation of father and son.

In Seneca's *Phaedra*, the central motif is nature and its opposite: 'Nature claims all for herself'. Stress is put on the unnatural sexual practices of Phaedra's family. Her mother Pasiphae has intercourse with a bull, and begets the Minotaur. Theseus abandoned her sister Ariadne after sex. So Venus, goddess of sexual love, curses their house. Yet Hippolytus hates sex.

When Phaedra conceives her illicit passion for Hippolytus, reason is defeated by that passion. So in Seneca, it is Phaedra, not the Nurse, who tells her stepson about it.

Imagery of the *hunt* is prominent in Seneca. At the play's start, Hippolytus is a hunter in control, in control of nature. But at the end, he is the hunted one, a prey to the unnatural monster from the sea. Here this creature symbolizes Phaedra's desire for Hippolytus. Parts of whose fragmentary body are collected by Theseus' men. Hippolytus' asexual nature is dissolved.

Racine's play *Phèdre* (1677) sums up Phaedra: 'Vénus toute entière à sa proie attachée, Venus completely bound to her prey.

ALCESTIS

Euripides' tragicomedy *Alcestis* (438) unusually took the place of the satyr play, and won second prize. Alcestis is a remarkable woman, very different from Medea, Antigone, and Phaedra.

Central to this play is the theme of Death (*Thanatos*), who appears as a character. Death is inevitable, its timing unknown. When the king Admetus requires someone to die instead of him, his elderly parents refuse to do so. But the king's wife Alcestis agrees to die. She stresses the topics of house, marriage, husband, children. The sort of things Athenian society prized. Pathos surrounds the death of Alcestis; Admetus and the children are deeply affected. As Thomas Mann wrote, 'A man's dying is more the survivors' affair than his own.' But in a startling reversal, the hero Herakles contrives to bring back Alcestis from the dead. His satiric aspect is his copious consumption of food and undiluted wine and his wearing a myrtle twig, symbol of Aphrodite, goddess of sex. All of which Herakles abandons when he realizes that Alcestis is dead. Here resurrection brings a new form of pleasure.

THE BACCHAE

Euripides' tragedy *The Bacchae*, which won first prize, was staged posthumously after 406, enacting a fierce contest between the king of Thebes, Pentheus (Grief), and the god Dionysus. It concerns two varieties of religion, sober reasonable for Pentheus, ecstatic emotional for Dionysus. The god's female worshippers, the Bacchae, epitomize the irrational element of Dionysus' religion: inhabiting the mountains, loving the dance, conjuring water, wine, honey. But for Pentheus they are devoted to sex and to drink.

The king protests too much. The god points out that to 'resist Dionysus is to resist the elemental in one's nature'. Excessive rationalism is a form of madness. And Pentheus' rejection of Dionysus is not supported by his grandfather Cadmus and the prophet Teiresias. Wine, after all, offers relief for the harshness of human life.

But the worship of Dionysus can be malevolent, can be violent, as when the Bacchae wound men with their wands; and when Agave, deranged, psychotic, kills her son Pentheus, in a parody of Greek animal sacrifice. Ignorant of who she is, Agave must undergo a form of psychotherapy that will provide her with the knowledge she lacks – with recognition (*anagnórisis*). Yet she and Cadmus must go into exile as scapegoats. Irrational religion, it seems, must be kept in check.

Meta-theatre is the most striking aspect of Euripides' technique in *The Bacchae*. Dionysus is the author of the drama, its stage director, its costume designer. So the god has the prurient king dress like a woman in full Bacchic regalia. Pentheus' gender identity is compromised; disaster looms.

LYSISTRATA

Lysistrata is one of five comedies of Aristophanes in which a resourceful heroine or hero brings about a triumph of fantasy over reality. Here and in *The Assembly Women*, women are prominent in the political life of Athens; as they could not be in real life. But this type of wit should not be confused with levity. The aim, says Horace, is 'to tell the truth with a smile'.

Lysistrata was staged in 411, when the war between Athens and Sparta had 7 years to run. After its disaster in Sicily, Athens was now in a very weak position. Lysistrata's plan is for the women of Greece to stage a sex strike, to continue until the men end the war. The slogan is 'Make love, not war'. Sterile forms of behaviour must be abandoned, life enhancing forms embraced. Lysistrata's name (Disbander of Armies) is close to that of Lysimache, contemporary priestess of Athena Polias, which suggests that she possesses authority.

Sex is prominent in Greek tragedy, but is treated in an elevated tone. Comedy treats sex in down-to-earth fashion, often obscene. So in a comic scene in *Lysistrata*, a man named Kenesias (Fucker) yearns to have sex with a woman named Myrrhine (Cunt). But this husband, erect, frustrated, consistently fails to do so.

More political is the seizure by the women of the Treasury on the Acropolis; this gives them control of the money used for the war.

Finally, the goddess Reconciliation appears – young, beautiful, and naked. Her contours suggest a map for terms of a truce. Male lust for her mirrors lust for reconciliation, for ending the war.

Lysistrata found a new resonance at the time of the Iraq War in 2003: in opposition to that war, it was performed, recited, lectured on, on 3 March, 2003 over 1,000 times.

ASSEMBLY WOMEN

Women take on an even greater role in male politics in Aristophanes' *Assembly Women* (about 391). The main political organ of Athens was the Assembly (*Ekklesia*), which consisted entirely of male citizens. Women, in this fantasy, disguised as men, take over and run the state – they are led by Praxagora (Effective Speaker) – because the men have presided over a disastrous state of affairs in Athens, a city defeated by Sparta in 404; ruled by pro-Spartan oligarchs; followed by an unusually moderate democracy.

Praxagora uses the metaphor of the ship of state: 'as things are at present, the ship's adrift: we're not getting anywhere'. Accordingly, the men 'voted to hand over control to the women', who are trained by Praxagora to adopt various male attributes such as speaking in public. Men are reduced to the level of the body: Blepyrus is constipated.

The most remarkable feature of the *Assembly Women* is its advocacy of a type of communism very similar to that found in Plato's *Republic* (can this be a coincidence?). Radical measures include a community of property, of wives, of children. Hence a young man pursues a young girl, but must fend off an old woman. A serious philosophical concept turns comic when part of a fantasy.

The play ends on a note of celebration (*Kómos*). Dinner with plenty of food, with choice wines, with dancing.

WOMEN AT THE THESMOPHORIA

The women in this comedy of Aristophanes take part in a religious harvest festival. It is for women only, and here the participants offer an eloquent account of themselves. They stress the manifold ways in which their husbands *control* them. In an instance of the male attack on them, the women produce 'Euripides' and his cousin' Mnesilochus, who is dressed as a woman in a yellow gown. This 'cousin' attributes every sort of misdemeanour to women: as with sex, as with wine.

The Athenian women are very hostile to Euripides, whom they want to kill: 'They say I slander them in my tragedies.' Medea and Phaedra might fit the bill. But not Alcestis, the women of Troy, the intellectual Melanippe. The faithful Penelope, it is pointed out, is missing from Euripides' oeuvre.

Euripides' private life is also fair game. A male dramatist, prominent or not, may not be above reproach. Euripides is, the women claim, an atheist, while *they* invoke a large number of Greek deities.

3 – MALE HEROES

The aim of the Greek hero is personal glory, not commitment to a cause. These men are special beings who achieve striking feats in war, in peace. But they are mortal, are constantly in danger, are liable to defeat. Indeed Yeats held that the hero discovers his mask in defeat.

Part of Lord Raglan's account of the *hero* is exemplified by Oedipus. His father is a king, who tries to kill his son at birth. The son is removed from his native land and raised by foster parents in a far country. As an adult, he returns to his place of birth. There the son kills a monster such as the Sphinx. He marries the queen, becomes king. Eventually, this king is expelled from the city, and meets a mysterious death.

The essential start of the Oedipus myth in Sophocles is an oracle of the prophetic god Apollo at Delphi, site of the chief religious authority of Greece. Mottoes on the god's temple were 'know thyself' and 'nothing to excess'. The oracle asserted that a male child, born to King Laius and Queen Jocasta of Thebes, would kill his father and marry his mother, thus violating two of society's central taboos. In a prior version of the myth, these things happened to Oedipus because of Laius' homosexual seduction of a boy. Why they happen in *King Oedipus* we do not know.

To avert parricide and incest, his parents expose the infant Oedipus on a mountain with a pin inserted in his foot to prevent him getting away. A Theban shepherd finds the child, and hands him over to a Corinthian shepherd. Oedipus grows up in Corinth with royal foster parents. Hearing of the oracle, he leaves Corinth and, at a crossroads, kills his father. In Thebes, Oedipus overcomes the monstrous Sphinx (head of a woman, body of a lion), and marries his mother. Because of toxic matter in Oedipus' life, a plague affects the city.

Yeats held that *King Oedipus* is 'the greatest masterpiece of Greek drama', one that provided 'a sense of the actual presence in a terrible sacrament of the god'. These views are enhanced by the play's brevity at 1453 lines, a brevity that suggests a detective story – with P.D. James pointing out that the aim of such fiction is 'the restoration of order'.

King Oedipus lays great stress on *knowledge*, with Oedipus a symbol of the human intelligence. He must find out who he is, what he has done. When he does find out (*recognition*), he is automatically ruined (*reversal*). No longer king, he blinds himself, a punishment for sexual crimes. His mother hangs herself.

Oedipus in this play is *dual* in a huge number of ways. Normally, duality in tragedy involves *two* people: Jason and Medea; Antigone and Creon; Philoctetes and Odysseus. Here it is just Oedipus.

Oedipus' name – Oidipous in Greek – is ambiguous. It can connote 'swollen foot', referring to the effect of the pin his parents abandoned him with at birth. It can also connote 'I know where'. Ironic, since he does *not* know his origins.

Oedipus has dual nationality: Theban by birth; Corinthian by upbringing. He starts off sighted without insight; he ends up blind with insight. Contrast Teiresias: always blind, always with insight.

Oedipus is transformed from king to nonentity.

There are three dual roles for Oedipus: detective and criminal; doctor and disease; hunter and quarry.

When Oedipus overcomes the Sphinx, he is the saviour of the city; when his crimes become known, he is its scapegoat – as when in the festival of Thargelia, Athens expelled people who were deemed to be scapegoats.

There are further dualities in *King Oedipus*. The Theban shepherd who found Oedipus was also with Laius when he was killed. The Corinthian shepherd who received Oedipus brings to him news of his supposed father's death. Dramatic irony occurs when Oedipus says of Laius 'I never saw him'. Romantic irony occurs when Oedipus says that he 'knows nothing'. It means that he has solved the riddle of the Sphinx about man, but is unaware he can't solve his own.

SENECA, *OEDIPUS*

This play stresses the fragility of life. Using the pathetic fallacy, in which non-human elements react to the life of human beings. The Chorus say, 'Everything is sharing in our suffering'. Oedipus says, 'I have made the heavens hurt us.' So there is no harvest, no water in rivers. Nature is overturned (*natura versa est*). More: Death is lethally contagious, with mourners at a funeral dropping dead around the corpse. Donne is pertinent: 'never send to know for whom the bell tolls; it tolls for thee'.

Seneca's *Oedipus* contains supernatural events not found in Sophocles. The oracle of Apollo about Oedipus' fate is not just referred to, but quoted, including the quarrel between his sons Polyneices and Eteocles. Major innovations in Seneca concern Teiresias. He has a helper in his daughter Manto (Prophesy), who is absent from *King Oedipus*.

But the most spectacular event in *Oedipus* is the appearance from the dead of the murdered Laius. In Sophocles, Laius is a pervasive, but non-physical presence. In Seneca, Laius is present on stage, and identifies Oedipus as guilty. Here Oedipus' self-knowledge is acquired by supernatural means, though not by the Roman practice of divination which has failed: little blood from a bull; a virgin heifer pregnant; wine changed to blood. The appearance in various guises of a Ghost is found in two other plays of Seneca, *Thyestes* and *Agamemnon*; and in Shakespeare, *Hamlet, Macbeth, Richard III*.

Seneca's ending is also different. The self-blinding of Oedipus is independent of Jocasta's suicide that comes later. That suicide, which suggests the Stoic suicide, takes place in front of the audience, whereas most acts of violence occur off-stage in Greek tragedy. In Seneca, Oedipus explicitly stresses that he is a scapegoat who takes upon himself the crimes of the city: 'I've paid due penalty'. No redemption.

SOPHOCLES, *OEDIPUS AT COLONUS*

This play, produced posthumously in 401, offers a valedictory celebration of Athens and of Oedipus. The setting at Colonus, one mile Northwest of Athens, is more important than in any other

Greek tragedy. There is praise for the locals, for the landscape. Compare in Plato's *Phaedrus* the Ilyssus in summer: fresh clear water; trees in full bloom; chorus of cicadas; shade from the sun. The Chorus in *Oedipus at Colonus* shower lavish praise on Colonus with its river Cephisus; on the glamour of horses; the singing of the nightingale; flowers like narcissus and crocus; the grey-leafed olive; on Deities like Athena patron goddess of Athens, who gave the city the major export of olive oil; on Poseidon, god of the sea, who provided horses and ships. Yeats went further: Colonus boasts a Platonic Form on earth that 'gives/Athenian intellect its mastery'.

When Oedipus arrives at Colonus he has lived through a catalogue of disasters. He is lame; perpetrator of parricide and incest; failed king; self-mutilated; scapegoat; exile. Oedipus comes first to the Wood of the Furies, a sacred place he is asked to leave. But Theseus, king of Athens, guarantees him protection, and he becomes an Athenian citizen. This begins his change of fortune. Oedipus now has friends and enemies. His daughters Antigone and Ismene support him. Others see Oedipus as a useful tool in their schemes. King Creon wants his body for Thebes, and carries off Oedipus' daughters, until they are rescued by Theseus. His son Polyneices wants Oedipus' help against his brother Eteocles.

These mundane matters are to be set aside. Oedipus cannot be a hero in the traditional sense like Achilles or Hector. But now he becomes a hero in the *religious* sense. Namely, 'a deceased person who exerts from the grave a power for good or evil and who demands appropriate honour' (Burkert). Such a person is linked to a particular place, here Colonus.

Announced by several claps of thunder, Oedipus' death in *Oedipus at Colonus* is miraculous: mysterious, secret, above all supernatural. As Oedipus says, 'I have been saved/for something great and terrible, something strange'. So he lies upon the earth between four sacred objects: hollow, rock, tomb, pear-tree. He is washed like the dead, sinks into the ground, observed only by Theseus, the precise mode of death unknown.

Tragedy very often ends with human death, that is disastrous; but Oedipus' death is supernatural, a triumph. But this positive ending is not, as in comedy, the union of man and woman. Rather, it is the union of hero and gods.

Is the real Oedipus complex his journey from disaster to success?

SOPHOCLES, *PHILOCTETES*

This is the only Greek tragedy without a woman in it. The question in Kyd's *The Spanish Tragedy* – 'For what's a play without a woman in it?' – requires the answer: 'quite a lot'.

Desmond Egan, the translator of *Philoctetes*, holds that Sophocles gives us 'that clear and steady gaze, that metaphysical honesty'; holds that this play explores 'some of the most profound issues touching on human life'.

When the Greeks were on their way to Troy, *Philoctetes* was bitten on the foot by a snake. Because his unhealed wound stank so much, the Greeks, persuaded by Odysseus, abandoned him on the deserted island of Lemnos. *Philoctetes* therefore lacks that crucial Greek entity, the city, *Polis*. After many years, the Trojan prophet Helenus revealed that Troy would not fall to the Greeks, unless Philoctetes were to be persuaded to fight with his invincible bow and arrows.

Sophocles' play concerns the efforts of Odysseus and Neoptolemus, son of Achilles, to get Philoctetes to come to Troy with them. But Philoctetes is an intransigent Sophoclean hero, one isolated both in the literal and metaphorical sense. Wronged by the Greeks, and especially by Odysseus, he is condemned to live a lonely painful existence. Compromise is a concept not in his vocabulary; hating his enemies is.

Of the two warriors to tackle Philoctetes, Odysseus is already the trickster of later tradition. He exemplifies a pejorative view of the Sophists and of Athenian demagogues. Words (*logoi*) are abused to further his aim. Odysseus is a moral relativist who believes that the end justifies the means. Orwell points out that political language 'is designed to make lies sound truthful'.

Unique to Sophocles is the use by Odysseus of the young Neoptolemus as intermediary – a warrior who is violent, but honourable. Initially, he is corrupted by Odysseus, deceives Philoctetes to get the bow, a powerful dramatic prop. Neoptolemus repents of his deceit, returns the bow, and decides to take Philoctetes to Greece (not Troy).

The change in Neoptolemus relates to the initiation process in the Athenian institution of the *ephebeia*, in which a young man becomes an adult at the age of 18, and undergoes military training. This young man expresses loyalty and solidarity. But he also expresses cunning. Neoptolemus in this play passes through the stages of the young man's initiation. First, he entraps Philoctetes with the language of deceit, a tricky *ephebe*. He then returns to his original Achillean self and proves loyal to his ephebic oath.

To break the impasse caused by Philoctetes' continuing intransigence, we need a *deus ex machina*. This is Herakles, original owner of the bow and arrows. He appears from the dead, announces that Zeus plans for Philoctetes to go to Troy. The hero acquiesces, takes part in Troy's fall and is healed. Another positive ending for Sophocles.

SOPHOCLES, *AJAX*

The warrior Ajax, son of Telamon, king of Salamis, was the leader of the Salaminians at Troy. Of giant size, of relentless courage, he kept leading the Greeks in attack with his elaborate body shield. Ajax became a local hero in Salamis.

In Sophocles' tragedy, *focalization* of Ajax is paramount. This term, that comes from the theory of narrative, refers to the point of view, the perspective from which events are described. So Ajax constantly presents his own views, and is constantly analysed by others. He emerges as ambivalent. On the one hand, full of energy, great in physique and spirit, self-sufficient. On the other hand, full of rage, tending to fail. Honour in *Ajax* is about who gets to possess the arms of the dead warrior Achilles. The contest is between Ajax and Odysseus. This is a striking example of how the Greeks loved a competition (*agón*) – one taking place not just in this play, but between this play and others in the City Dionysia.

Odysseus wins the competition. Ajax is angry, treats Odysseus as an enemy, seeks revenge. Violent hostility is directed not at the Trojans, but at a fellow Greek. A special type of civil war (*stasis*). The intransigence of Ajax is questioned by his concubine Tecmessa: 'by the gods, become softer' – just as Volumnia says to her son Coriolanus in Shakespeare: 'You are too absolute'.

The war goddess Athena, who is the enemy of Troy, cannot allow Ajax to kill Odysseus. The triumph of one leads to the downfall of the others. So Athena destroys Ajax by tricking him into killing animals instead of Odysseus. Unable to live with dishonour, Ajax decides on suicide. At one point, he appears to relent, but then kills himself. He is the only Homeric warrior to do so. This violent act takes place on stage, unlike most such acts in Greek tragedy.

After one contest ends in disaster, another acrimonious contest about the burial of Ajax follows. The Greek leaders Agamemnon and Menelaus oppose burial. Odysseus favours it, and prevails. As *Antigone* shows, proper burial of a dead person was crucial for the Greeks. Shakespeare in *Titus Andronicus* sums up this issue:

> The Greeks upon advice did bury Ajax
> That slew himself, and wise Laertes' son
> Did graciously plead for his funeral.

There is irony here: Odysseus becomes the champion of Ajax in death.

EURIPIDES, *HERAKLES*

Herakles is the greatest Greek hero, but not at all typical. He is the mighty son of Zeus; he is also a god. Being for Pindar a 'hero-god', Herakles straddles the three realms of existence. He lives on earth; visits the underworld; inhabits the world of the gods. He does not elude death, but he has no grave. Herakles eventually became famous for his Twelve Labours, including the cleansing of the Augean stables, and the apples of the Hesperides.

Herakles enjoys power, especially power over dangerous animals such as the bull, the lion, and the serpent. He engages in a struggle with Centaurs and Amazons. Herakles is the official ancestor of the Dorian kings, a prototype of the ruler. But this hero can also be subservient: he becomes the slave of the Lydian queen Omphale, and is dressed like a woman; he is driven mad by the goddess Hera. He is subject, too, to gluttony and lust.

Astonishing reversals dominate Euripides' play *Herakles*. For Aristotle, reversal in tragedy involved a person moving from a good to a bad situation. Euripides is large, contains multitudes of complex reversals.

Herakles has been away in the underworld in pursuit of the dog Cerberus. In his absence, the usurper Lycus seizes power in Thebes; this character is invented in Euripides. Lycus wants to kill Herakles' wife Megara and their three children, but in one of the play's startling reversals it is Lycus who is killed by Herakles, back from the underworld.

So far, Herakles is on top. But another reversal is to come. The goddess Hera is angry because Alcmena, another woman of her husband Zeus, is the mother of Herakles. Hera renders Herakles mad, so that, in a striking piece of irony, it is he who kills Megara and the children. There is a final twist in this complex plot. Herakles recovers his sanity, and is protected by Theseus, king of Athens, whom he had delivered from the underworld. He goes to Athens to be cleansed of pollution. This means redemption for Herakles and a coup for Athens.

Euripides does not do simple.

SENECA, *THE MADNESS OF HERCULES*

The cult of Hercules came to Rome at an early date. Here he was the god of victory and of commercial enterprise, with an altar in the cattle market. In Roman myth, Hercules killed the fire-breathing monster Cacus. This hero was adopted by the politician Mark Antony and by the Emperor Commodus.

Seneca's play *The Madness of Hercules* has a different opening to Euripides' Herakles: a lengthy speech by the goddess Juno (Greek Hera), showing her to be seemingly complaisant about her husband's affairs. 'I have abandoned Jupiter to all his other girls.' But in reality 'my hate will never end'.

Seneca has the usurper Lycus seeking to woo Megara. A major innovation not found in Euripides. Marriage to Lycus will provide him with legitimacy: 'But a nice big royal wedding/and bed with Megara, will make our powers/flow together.' This mirrors the political marriages of the Roman aristocracy. But Megara is having none of it: 'Hercules, I will die yours'. She is like a Roman *univira*, a woman who remains faithful to one man. When rejected, Lycus wishes a single fire to consume Megara and her children. This wooing scene in Seneca effected a striking impact upon Shakespeare in *Richard III*. Clever, witty, devious, Richard gets Anne to marry him, despite the fact that he has killed her father and her husband. For Kott, it is 'one of the greatest scenes written by Shakespeare, and one of the greatest ever written'. Seneca cannot be too heavy.

The remainder of Seneca's play follows Euripides. Herakles kills Lycus; is driven mad; murders his wife and children. Then Theseus gives him sanctuary in Athens. When Macbeth reflects on the ruin of his life, he closely follows Seneca's Hercules:

I have lived long enough: my way of life
Is fall'n into the sere, the yellow leaf;
And that which should accompany old age,
As honour, love, obedience, troops of friends
I must not look to have ... .

SOPHOCLES, *WOMEN OF TRACHIS*

Herakles lives in Trachis (the female Chorus is from there). He has been absent for 15 months, so that his son Hyllus is sent to find him. Herakles has told his wife Deianeira that his crisis would come after that, either to die or to enjoy a happy life.

Several Greek themes occur in *Women of Trachis*: Return, *nostos*, when Herakles comes home after the sack of a city in Euboea. Concubine: he brings with him Iole, with whom he has fallen in love. Compare Agamemnon who comes home from Troy with Cassandra. More: in both cases, a spouse will die: Agamemnon, Herakles.

Herakles is now involved with two women; this is a love triangle, Herakles, Deianeira, Iole. Deianeira aims to ruin her husband's love, so she sends him a love charm that is smeared on a robe (given to her by the dying Centaur Nessus). But this robe turns out to be poisonous. Deianeira has made, without meaning to, a ghastly mistake (*hamartia*), the consequence of which is the death of Herakles, whereas Medea deliberately poisons her rival Glauké with a robe.

The result of all this is drastic. Herakles is to be burnt on a pyre on Mount Oeta (the Latin play about that is probably not by Seneca). Deianeira kills herself. Hyllus, son of Herakles, is required to marry Iole. Death often ends tragedy, comedy often ends in marriage. But in *Women in Trachis*, these events are complex. Herakles' death was accidental. Deianeira commits suicide because of that accident. Hyllus' marriage is forced, and not to a women of his class.

Ezra Pound made very high claims for *Women of Trachis*, of which he wrote a version. It is 'the highest peak of Greek sensibility registered in any of the plays that have come down to us'. So much for other plays by Sophocles: *King Oedipus*, *Antigone*. Hyllus, at the end of *Women of Trachis*, views the gods as malevolent, merciless, arbitrary. When in conclusion, he asserts, 'And all you have seen is Zeus', this is no apologia for the gods. Rather, the assertion hovers between resignation and anger. Rejecting his own well-known sentence 'what SPLENDOUR IT ALL COHERES', Pound later admitted that he himself was not up to chronicling coherence: 'And I am not a demi-god,/I cannot make it cohere'.

EURIPIDES, *CHILDREN OF HERAKLES*

This is not one of the better known Greek tragedies. But its depiction of a cruel, immoral world means that it 'may yet prove a tragedy whose time has come' (Hall).

Children of Herakles concerns that most contemporary of issues, refugees. The king of Tiryns in the Argive plain, Eurystheus, required Herakles to perform Twelve Labours in expiation for the murder of his family. Here Eurystheus desires to kill by stoning Herakles' children, illustrating the Greek belief in harming your enemies.

The children seek sanctuary from Argos at Marathon near Athens as a group of suppliants. In history, both Athens and Sparta abused the rights of suppliants, and these instances are exploited by the two sides at the start of the Peloponnesian War. *Athens*: in mid-sixth century, Cylon and his fellow conspirators took refuge in the temple of Athena, but were nearly all killed. *Sparta*: the king Cleomenes I (about 520-490) set on fire thousands of Argives in a sacred grove. History mirrors myth: violence is ever present. There is violence when, in a very shocking moment, the Argive herald proves capable of using force against the children of Herakles. The proper job of a herald was not to be partisan, but to negotiate between opposing sides. There is even more violence, when human sacrifice is required to achieve the success of Athens as the Argive army advances. What is most poignant about this is that the victim, Macaria, daughter of Herakles, is willing to die, and does so.

Iolaus, Herakles' nephew, is a champion of the children. He undergoes a transformation unique in Greek tragedy: from a feeble old man to a virile warrior. Another surprise: freedom to a slave is promised by Alcmena, Herakles' mother, when he reports the victory of Athens over Eurystheus. But Alcmena reverts to normal heroic mode when she orders the death of Eurystheus.

4 – THE HOUSE OF ATREUS AND THE TROJAN WAR

Revenge is a concept, an emotion that is central to the persons of the House of Atreus, and to the persons engaged in the Trojan War. Revenge is central also to a significant number of English tragedies written between the 1590's and the 1630's, beginning with Kyd's *The Spanish Tragedy*, and including Shakespeare's *Titus Andronicus* and *Hamlet*. Seneca's tragedies are an important and very obvious antecedent for these bloodthirsty plays, providing the theme of evil in the ruler, the theme of a Ghost calling for revenge. Thomas Nashe noted the impact of the translations of Seneca into English in 1581:

> English Seneca read by candlelight yields many good sentences, as *Blood is a beggar* and so forth; and if you entreat him fair to a frosty morning, he will afford you whole Hamlets – I should say handfuls of tragic speeches.

That is: a revenge play that includes aphorisms and rhetorical speeches.

Revenge arises when A commits an injury, typically murder, against B. B will then avenge, in due course, this outrage. Toxic matter from the past must be eliminated. But sometimes that is not enough: a vendetta comes into play. A notable example occurs in the House of Atreus. This type of revenge constitutes, in Bacon's famous phrase, 'wild justice'. Not sanctioned by public law, but perpetrated by an individual person of their own accord. As the Viceroy of Portugal says in *The Spanish Tragedy*, 'They reck no laws that meditate revenge'.

In *Titus Andronicus*, when Titus kills Alarbus, eldest son of Tamora, queen of the Goths, she asserts 'I am Revenge'. Her other sons rape and mutilate Titus' daughter Lavinia, and kill her husband Bassianus.

SENECA, *THYESTES*

The house of Atreus is a highly dysfunctional family, among the many such in Greek mythology. The vendetta occurring in this family originates in a curse. The myth runs as follows. Pelops, son of Tantalus, sought to marry Hippodameia, daughter of Oenomaus, king of Elis. He would win her by outdistancing the king in a chariot race. Pelops bribed Myrtilus, the king's charioteer, to nobble his master's chariot, with the result that Oenomous was thrown off and killed. Pelops then married Hippodameia, but he refused to give Myrtilus his reward, and threw him into the sea. The dying Myrtilus cursed Pelops. This is the origin of the curse on the house of Atreus.

A curse that manifests itself in Pelops' sons, the brothers Atreus and Thyestes. In Seneca's *Thyestes*, Atreus becomes a very clear example of evil in the ruler (the subtext is the behaviour of Julio-Claudian Emperors like Nero). Evil that is effected because of revenge. Thyestes seduces Atreus' wife Aeropé, and is banished by his brother. Later, Atreus invites Thyestes back to Mycenae, alleging he is prepared to share power. But Atreus exacts a brutal revenge: he kills Thyestes' three sons, and serves them to their father in a cannibal meal. So Atreus' passion defeats reason as advocated by the attendant.

Atreus believes that revenge is a duty, and it becomes an expression of his personality, devoted to desire and appetite. To justify this, Atreus turns into a virtuoso rhetorician, an egotist par excellence. His aphorism is 'You cannot say you have executed a crime, unless you better it' – an aphorism known to Macbeth after the murder of Duncan and the planned murder of Banquo and Fleance: 'Things bad begun make strong themselves by ill.' The Chorus offers a different kind of ethics. They hold the stoic view that political power is false kingship; true kingship involves controlling your soul.

The actions of Atreus turn the world upside down. The impossible happens in a striking version of the pathetic fallacy: the sun disappears. Gone then is the love that moves the sun and the other stars; Atreus traffics in hate and mocks civilization by turning the ritual of animal sacrifice, a social occasion, into a bloody and obscene private murder.

The Chorus asks 'Will the last days come in our time?' Answer: 'Yes'. For Atreus this means that the gods are no longer of any account: 'I dismiss the gods; the summit of my prayers is reached'. An egregious example of solipsism, but one that Atreus gets away with. Is Beckett any bleaker than this?

But Thyestes is not completely innocent. Like Atreus, he wants political power, seduced by wealth and comfort. He is no stoic sage. He is unable to keep faith with his stated principles. He has lost his soul.

Thyestes begins with the Ghost of Tantalus, grandfather of Atreus and Thyestes, who served the flesh of his son Pelops to the gods. There is also Fury, who avenges crimes with the family. Fury expresses a very jaundiced and pessimistic view of the world, a world that is corrupt and evil, a world that includes the *anger* of Atreus. In such a world, there is no room for hope. There is only what the Chorus call 'this endless cycle of catastrophe'.

Caryl Churchill, the translator of *Thyestes*, links that play to the revenge tragedy of *Hamlet*: Hamlet 'wants to be a hero in a Senecan play. I didn't know that till I read *Thyestes*'.

EURIPIDES, *IPHIGENEIA IN AULIS*

This play deals with events before the Trojan War between the Greeks and the Trojans; it is incomplete, and some of it is spurious.

That Troy was a real and wealthy city in North West Turkey was established by Heinrich Schliemann in the 1870's, who claimed, rightly, to have opened up a whole new world of archaeology. Troy's many layers included those in the Late Bronze Age. The city designated Troy VIIA was destroyed by force in the period 1230-1190/80. This and similar events could provide a certain basis in history for Homer's account in the *Iliad* of the Trojan War.

Greek myth finds Helen, wife of Menelaus king of Sparta, the cause of the Trojan War. In the company of Paris, prince of Troy, she goes with him to his home. This transfer of Helen is open to interpretation. Did she go willingly? Was she abducted? Is Eros, sexual desire, to blame? Whatever of these explanations, the war was more likely to have been caused by political and commercial considerations.

The Greeks had to get Helen back by attacking Troy. But a serious obstacle prevented the fleet from sailing across the Aegean from Aulis on the east coast of Greece. This was the anger of the very complex goddess Artemis – anger caused by the Greek leader Agamemnon killing a stag in Artemis' sacred grove, anger to be propitiated by the stark remedy of sacrificing Agamemnon's daughter Iphigeneia. In *Iphigeneia in Aulis*, this sacrifice allows the Greeks to go to war. Human sacrifice did exist in Greece. The Athenians killed Persian prisoners before the battle of Salamis (480). A person could be killed in the worship of Dionysus, as Pentheus in Euripides' *Bacchae*.

Agamemnon here is faced with an impossible choice, a no-win situation. The Greeks can get to Troy only if he presides over the appalling crime of filicide. If he rejects that act, the Greeks are unable to go to Troy, and honour will be lost. This is not the *aporia* of philosophy, failure to achieve a result. Rather, whatever Agamemnon's decision, there will be a disastrous result.

Endless *change of mind* is the essential characteristic of the persons in *Iphigeneia in Aulis*. This applies to Agamemnon, Menelaus, Achilles, Iphigeneia herself. They fail to be consistent about the fate of Iphigeneia: should she die or live? Whitman seems apposite: 'do I contradict myself? Very well, I contradict myself.' But Whitman's further assertion that he 'contains multitudes' does not apply here: people have just *two* options. So Athens in history changed its mind about the fate of Mytilene in 427. The decision of the Assembly to execute all the male inhabitants was reversed the next day.

Agamemnon
First, he rejects the killing of Iphigeneia. Then he summons her to say she must die in a fictitious marriage to Achilles (who is ignorant of this): 'Hades, it seems, will soon marry her.' But Agamemnon cancels the summons.
Menelaus
First, he supports the supposed marriage. Then he offers to give up the expedition.
Agamemnon
He now, fearing the army, favours sacrificing Iphigeneia.

Achilles

Knowing of the deception, he now seeks to save Iphigeneia.

Iphigeneia

Aristotle finds her 'inconsistent': 'as a suppliant she is quite unlike what she is later'. From trying to save herself, she offers her body for Greece, as an adolescent faced with adult power might.

Clytemnestra

The one person who does not waver in her support for her daughter is her mother. She recalls that Agamemnon has form in filicide: he murdered a previous baby of hers (an invention of Euripides).

The military men Iphigeneia has to deal with are lying, shameless, self-centred, full of bluster, and with a selective memory. In Euripides' play, the demands of *society* have triumphed over those of the *family*. War looms that, ironically, is held to safeguard a different Greek family.

EURIPIDES AND SENECA, *THE TROJAN WOMEN*

The catastrophic end of Troy and its civilization is the theme of these two tragedies. The city is totally destroyed, burnt. The male leaders are killed. The royal women of Troy are to become sexual slaves in Greece. As Queen Hecuba says, 'Troy, unhappy Troy, you no longer exist'. An earthquake makes the point. And yet, and yet: the women of obliterated Troy are given a *voice* by Euripides, by Seneca.

Euripides' play was staged in Athens in 415. The subtext is the barbaric treatment by Athens in 416 of the small island of Melos in the southwest Aegean. Melos was a Spartan colony that remained neutral in the Peloponnesian War. Athens required the island to ally itself with its Empire, but Melos refused. Athens then captured Melos, killed the men and enslaved the women and children. Its ruthless policy was set forth in Thucydides' Melian Dialogue. Finley sums up: 'Athenian imperialism employed all the forms of exploitation that were available and possible in that society.' But tragedy questions ideology, though through a distancing mechanism.

The Greek herald Talthybius tells the Trojan women to which Greek warrior they are assigned. It is natural for them to baulk at this. Given to Odysseus, Hecuba labels him 'a foul man of trickery'. Andromache expresses a scathing paradox: 'O you

Greeks, you who have devised atrocities worthy of barbarians'. Ethnic roles are reversed. The Greeks see the Trojans as barbarians, but the term applies to them: it is the Trojans who are civilized. More startling, more complex still is the situation of Cassandra who exhibits a psychotic acceptance of herself as clandestine bride to Agamemnon.

Euripides stages debate between Helen and Hecuba about who is to blame for the Trojan War. This is at root about ethics: how are human beings to live? Hecuba believes Helen did not act in an ethical way; a woman attacking another woman. But Helen is a practised rhetorician, and launches an ingenious counter-attack. Blame is cast everywhere: on Hecuba and Priam, parents of Paris; on Paris himself; on the goddess Aphrodite. But at this point, her husband Menelaus wants to kill Helen.

Gods do indeed have a role to play in Euripides. As often, they quarrel among themselves: Poseidon blames Hera and Athena for the destruction of Troy. But Athena changes sides, and helps Poseidon ensure that the Greeks have a difficult voyage home.

Seneca's play also has a subtext – that of the Julio-Claudian Emperors of Rome, and especially Nero. Despotic, murderous, with grandiose tendencies, Nero committed suicide in 68. Chaos followed in Rome, mirroring that of Troy.

Troy is finished. But the Greeks are afraid that one day it may rise again; afraid of the Trojan princess Polyxena, because she could give birth to a fresh generation of Trojan warriors; afraid of Astyanax, son of Hector and Andromache, because he could become such a Trojan warrior. Two threats to be exterminated. In Seneca, Agamemnon is the voice of Reason, and rejects more bloodshed as in the killing of Polyxena. But Pyrrhus, son of Achilles, wants her dead, mocking Agamemnon for the killing of Iphigeneia. In the event, the Greek prophet Calchas endorses the deaths of Polyxena and Astyanax.

In Seneca, Helen clashes with Andromache, who castigates Helen as 'an abomination, an infection, and a pollution'. Helen tries self-pity: she is enslaved, she mourns Paris. But she will help the Greeks kill Polyxena in an act at the tomb of Achilles, troped as a perverse and bizarre 'marriage'. In Euripides, this killing of Polyxena has taken place before the action of *The Trojan Women* (it occurs in his *Hecuba*). But in Seneca the deaths of both Polyxena and Astyanax form the climax of the play.

Significant in this climax is a marked amount of the meta-theatrical. What is happening is like a stage performance: 'like a theatre'; 'the final act', the crowd 'watch'.

The Trojan Women of Euripides and of Seneca are plays much possessed by death, so that the tragedy of Euripides becomes 'a timeless indictment of the horror and futility of all wars' (Hamilton).

AESCHYLUS, *ORESTEIA*

Swinburne said that *The Oresteia* is 'the greatest spiritual work of man'. Winning first prize in 458, *The Oresteia* is the only complete trilogy of Athenian tragedy we possess. It is made up of *Agamemnon*, *The Libation Bearers* and *Eumenides* that deal with a connected theme, the House of Atreus. The plot seems simple: continuous revenge in the vendetta of that family.

In brief: back from Troy, Agamemnon is killed by his wife Clytemnestra and her lover Aegisthus. Their son Orestes, supported by their daughter Electra, kills Clytemnestra and Aegisthus. But the vendetta comes to an end, when Orestes is acquitted in a law court in Athens.

But *The Oresteia* raises complex issues: how the individual person acts in society, how the matters of Responsibility and Justice are interrogated. Justice (*Dike*) seems to lie with the person who demands Revenge. For Clytemnestra it is revenge for the murder by Agamemnon of their daughter Iphigeneia, together with his bringing back a concubine, Cassandra. For Orestes, it is revenge for the killing of his father. Earlier, for Menelaus, it is revenge for the abduction of his wife Helen. If one word encapsulates what is going on here, it is 'blood'; a synecdoche for the murdered body. The Chorus in *The Libation Bearers* asserts that 'when blood of slaughter/wets the ground it wants more blood'. Macbeth, after the murder of Banquo, states 'It will have blood, they say, blood will have blood.'

The murder of Agamemnon comes about after he has walked upon purple tapestries. Purple, in the Greco-Roman world, was a colour associated with power, political power – as with Roman and Byzantine Emperors, such as Constantine, who had the title 'Born to the Purple'. Agamemnon knows that he would be guilty of arrogance (*hubris*) by stepping on the god's purple, by expecting to be treated like a god. But Clytemnestra, with considerable skill, coaxes him into doing precisely that.

Agamemnon's death is not, as is usual, reported by a Messenger. In a lengthy, vivid and radical scene, Cassandra, who is the priestess of Apollo, predicts his murder. The term 'blood' is again to the fore: 'The whole house reeks of blood' – as in the past with Atreus; as now with Agamemnon; as in the future with Clytemnestra. It is a woman who is absolutely ruthless.

When Orestes kills his mother, the crime of matricide, he is pursued by the Furies, female deities who avenge murder within the family. But they do not kill Orestes: wild justice yields to the justice of a court of law in Athens: the Areopagus that tried cases of homicide. The Furies prosecute; Apollo defends. When the votes are equal, Athena supports Orestes, ensuring he is acquitted (as was Athenian practice). To copper fasten the new order, the Furies, renamed the Eumenides or Kindly Ones, are incorporated into Athenian society.

Civilization, it seems, triumphs over savagery. But the matter is not so simple. Equal votes suggest ambivalence. Athena's position is equivocal. Since she was born from the head of Zeus, she has no mother, and since she is a virgin, she has no child. Yet it is a trial of *matricide* that she presides over.

Aeschylus, arbitrary 'Justice', and the god Zeus are invoked by Hardy in the fatalistic conclusion to his novel *Tess of the D'Urbervilles* (1891). Tess was abandoned by her husband; was previously raped by another man, whom she, finally, murdered; was then hanged: 'Justice' was done, and the President of the Immortals, in Aeschylean phrase, had ended his sport with Tess – as happened with Agamemnon, with Clytemnestra, though not with Orestes.

EURIPIDES, *HECUBA*

This is a very bleak play. Two of Hecuba's children – her daughter Polyxena and her son Polydorus – are killed. Hecuba exacts revenge for the death of her son; changing from victim to avenger. The ghost of Achilles demands the sacrifice of Polyxena. After some debate among the Greeks, Odysseus leads her away – a very unattractive figure: cunning, populist, shameful. He ignores Hecuba's plea for her daughter. Ignores her reminder that he once owed his life to her (while, allegedly, a spy in the Trojan camp). Doing good to a friend is not, for Odysseus, an ethical doctrine.

Polyxena's death, which is graphically described, is one she accepts willingly. She dies as a free woman. She will not live as a slave.

More disaster is heaped on Hecuba: the murder of Polydorus. She has entrusted him for safekeeping to Polymestor, king of the Thracian Chersonese (the Dardanelles). This man by killing Polydorus exhibits the perceived vices of the Thracians: greed, cowardice, savagery. Polymestor has abused the reciprocal obligation of a guest-friend (*xenos*), in order to gain possession of a vast amount of gold that Hecuba left with him. Lust for money may not be the root of all evils, but it is certainly the root of this one. And, as Hecuba points out, power corrupts.

Polydorus' corpse was thrown into the sea, and so lacks a proper burial (cf. *Antigone*). When it is brought to Hecuba, it suffices to turn her into a violent avenger, but one not actively supported by Agamemnon, though he is sympathetic. Hecuba and her women lure Polymestor to her tent. Then they tear out his eyes, a fate that, in Byzantine times, rendered a man unfit to be Emperor. They also kill two of Polymestor's sons to ensure there will be no continuity of line. These violent acts can be justified by the mythical practice of revenge, but also by aspects of Attic law. More: when Hecuba is turned into a bitch, and her tomb becomes 'Dog's tomb', this is a landmark that saves ships.

Hamlet cites Hecuba's reaction to her suffering, as he castigates an over-enthusiastic actor:

> 'What's Hecuba to him, or he to Hecuba,
> That he should weep for her?

EURIPIDES, *ANDROMACHE*

This is a play perhaps written for the royal house of Molossia in Epirus, North West Greece.

After the fall of Troy, Andromache is assigned to Neoptolemus in Thessaly as concubine. But he is married to Hermione, daughter of Menelaus, king of Sparta. So we have a *ménage à trois*, with all the complexities of such a situation. Friendship between two females does not exist in Greek tragedy. Here enmity does. Arising out of the fact that Hermione is jealous of her rival Andromache – an emotion that can uniquely, says Proust, 'train the writer's mind'. So Hermione asks, 'Isn't sex the most important thing for women?' She expects the answer 'Yes'.

The sexual situation in *Andromache* crystalizes in the matter of children. Marriage for a woman in fifth century Athens existed for 'the ploughing of legitimate children'. Here Andromache and Neoptolemus have a son named Molossus out of wedlock. But the married Hermione has no child, a state she blames on her rival. Leading Hermione and her father Menelaus to want to kill Andromache and Molossus. A woman scorned, intent on revenge.

The Chorus are pessimistic: only in death can you call a human being happy. But *Andromache* ends on a positive note. When Neoptolemus is killed by Orestes, he takes Hermione away (being previously engaged to her). The goddess Thetis, a *dea ex machina*, ensures that her husband Peleus becomes a god. Andromache is to marry Helenus, son of Priam and Hecuba, which seems to turn *Andromache* into a tragicomedy.

SOPHOCLES AND EURIPIDES, *ELECTRA*

The vendetta in these plays moves on a generation, the children of Clytemnestra kill her to avenge her murder of their father Agamemnon. Electra is another of Sophocles' intransigent characters. For Virginia Woolf, she 'stands before us like a figure so tightly bound that she can only move an inch this way, or an inch that'. The focalization of Electra is made overt by the fact that she has one of the longest speaking parts in Greek tragedy.

Electra constantly mourns Agamemnon: O'Neill's play is called *Mourning Becomes Electra*. Clytemnestra disapproves, so that mother and daughter exchange abuse in the language of the law courts. The fictitious death of Orestes in a chariot race is reported by a Tutor, in the longest set piece in the plays of Sophocles. Very much alive, he is here for vengeance, revealing his identity to Electra. Clytemnestra is ignorant of this, but dreams Orestes has returned to life.

Orestes kills his mother (off stage). Her death cries suggest those of Agamemnon: the murders are equal. Aegisthus is also killed. In Aeschylus, Orestes feels guilt about matricide; in Sophocles, he does not. Matricide is accepted, is a given, part of what happens.

In a major innovation, the Electra of Euripides marries a poor farmer, who is not even given a name (under lexicalization). Deprived of her royal background, Electra chooses to perform menial tasks (carrying water), while dressed in rags and with filthy hair. Her marriage is not consummated.

Things are problematic in the *Electra* of Euripides. The ethics of killing Clytemnestra are far from clear. The Delphic Oracle approves, but Castor, brother of Clytemnestra, does not. In any case, Orestes arrives at the farm, intent on murder. But now there is another discordant note. Euripides parodies The *Libation Bearers* of Aeschylus, in which the kinship of Orestes and Electra is established, because, allegedly, they have the same size in boots. Orestes disputes this 'fact' – as does, with irony, Joyce: 'in ancient Greece brothers and sisters took the same size in boots'.

The tit-for-tat killing of the vendetta proceeds. As Electra makes clear to Orestes about their mother: 'kill her as she killed your father and mine'. So Clytemnestra and Aegisthus are murdered by Orestes, and displayed on a machine.

But this is by no means the conclusion of the play. There are positive notes. Electra is given to Pylades, friend of Orestes. Driven by the Furies to Athens and tried for matricide, Orestes in acquitted, which is more Aeschylus than Sophocles.

5 – ARISTOPHANES AND THE CITY OF ATHENS

The contemporary city of Athens is the subject of Aristophanes' plays. Aristotle held that 'the city is in nature prior to households and each of us individually'. The city was the place in which the good life was possible.

A highly idealized analysis of the political system of Athens is outlined by the leader Pericles in his Funeral speech of 430, as recorded by Thucydides (2.35-46). Here Athens is a unique, free and tolerant democracy, so that its (male) citizens should become its 'lovers'. Bacon believed that hyperbole is 'comely in nothing but love'. Certainly not in politics, even if politics is troped as love.

The comedies of Aristophanes are an antidote to this kind of pernicious rhetoric. Above all, he could exploit the Peloponnesian War between Athens and Sparta (431-04) by mocking it. By mocking, too, other aspects of life in fifth century Athens: tragic drama, philosophy, jury service. Real people are insulted: Kleon, Socrates, Euripides. Aristophanes' mode in the comedies is that of *satire*; Athenian life is, without mercy, attacked for all its vices and follies. Crucially lacking is self-knowledge.

But Athens in the fifth century allowed for *dissent*. Writers of tragedy and of comedy were free to critique aspects of prevailing ideology. For all that, Aristophanes' comedies often have a satisfactory ending (*kómos*). Rebirth goes with the territory. What we do not find in these plays is the depiction of romantic love between boy and girl. This becomes a stock theme only in the later comedy of Menander (342–about 292) and others.

To this day, the city provides artists with material, allows them to dissent. George Gissing says, 'I am bound to be in London because I must work at gathering some new material.' Experimental Modernism was very often the art of polyglot cities, with Paris at its centre. And Aristophanes makes an appearance.

In Eliot's radical and unfinished verse drama *Sweeney Agonistes* (1926-7; 1932), which was admired by Brecht, the subtitle is 'Fragments of an Aristophanic melodrama'. Aristophanes' comedies and melodrama share an element of the sensational and a satisfactory ending. Both Eliot and Aristophanes employ the contemporary city: for Eliot, a shabby flat in London, with characters based on real people. Characters who discuss murder.

ARISTOPHANES, *THE FROGS*

This comedy was staged at the Lenaia in 405 and, in a unique event, staged again in 404. The play presents a spectacular instance of the meta-theatrical: a contest between the dead dramatists Aeschylus and Euripides, which is presided over by the god of the theatre, Dionysus. Such a contest (*agón*) between two dramatists ensures that Sophocles can be left out; he is 'peaceable'. The aim is to find out which man can 'save the city'. Athens was now in a very bad state. Defeat in the Peloponnesian War was imminent; there was difficulty with the food supply; there was acute tension between democrats and oligarchs.

Art is here seen as *didactic*. A modern example is the plays of Shaw: he advocated his views on every possible topic. The opposite tendency is found in Shakespeare: his strategic opacity means that we do not know what he believed about anything. When the artist tackles politics, to teach becomes even more problematic. Charlotte Brontë said, 'I cannot write books handling the topics of the day.'

What, then, does art, including drama, give us? Walsh argues that literature 'provides knowledge in the form of realization: the realization of what anything might come to as a form of lived experience'. For Aristophanes, this realization involves a knowledge of what is *wrong* with Athens, so that the mode must be *attack*. As Juvenal wrote, 'anger produces verse'.

In the contest between Aeschylus and Euripides, their style – or alleged style – is crucial. It is paramount for writers: Joyce believed that the only important thing is style. Euripides finds

Aeschylus has an obscure, inflated style, with ludicrously long words. Euripides claims to have a down-to-earth style. In reality, both dramatists employ a form of Greek that is far removed from demotic speech (especially in the Choral Odes). One item of style is especially prominent: Aeschylus mocks Euripides' Prologues by claiming he finished each line with the tag 'lost his oilflask'. The force of this phrase, which is repeated 7 times, is that it becomes funny because it is so often repeated.

Morality. Aeschylus' claims are these. His own plays taught Athenians to be brave, disciplined, honourable. Those of Euripides taught Athenians to be cowardly, disputatious, immoral. This is a crude instance of the didactic approach, validated because of its comic hyperbole.

One concrete example of politics comes up: what to do about the maverick politician Alcibiades, who is 'an acutely unstable combination of ego-defined with society-defined ambitions' (Davies). A man who fought for Athens, then for Sparta, then for Athens again, as Euripides indicates. Aeschylus is more to the point: it is not wise to rear within the city a lion's whelp, but, if this happens, the city must tolerate its ways.

Dionysus at the beginning of *The Frogs* favoured Euripides. But at the end, he announces: 'I have declared Aeschylus is the winner.' In a sense, both dramatists get their due.

Much of *The Frogs* presents a comic portrayal of the chameleon god Dionysus. Plato objected to accounts of the gods that saw them as engaging in seriously immoral acts. But it is possible for Aristophanes to mock Dionysus in a play put on at one of the god's festivals. This is not irreverent, it is fun. Quite different from the portrayal of the gods in tragedy.

The Chorus of Initiates into one of the Mystery religions is very positive about the human condition. This note of celebration relates to the fact that the initiates – and their clones – can expect a happy afterlife. Excluded are mockers, party politicians, traitors.

ARISTOPHANES, THE ACHARNIANS, THE KNIGHTS, PEACE

These three plays were staged in the opening years of the Peloponnesian War: respectively, in 425; 424; 421. Wilfred Owen, writing about World War I, said, 'My subject is war, and the pity of war.' It is the tragic mode, as in Euripides' *The Trojan*

Women. But Aristophanes employs the comic mode, so that war becomes ridiculous.

The background to *The Acharnians* is that, at the start of the war, Athens allowed the Spartans to ravage the countryside of Attica, to destroy corn, vines, olive trees. People living there were moved into the city of Athens, so that overcrowding became a problem.

In *The Acharnians*, a poor farmer named Dikaiopolis (Just Citizen) is unhappy that no peace is being made. So he decides, in a fantastic way, to negotiate a private, not a state, treaty. One for himself, his wife, his kids. When Dikaiopolis asserts, 'I've never run for office', Athenian ideology viewed such disdain for the public life of politics as reprehensible. But for Dikaiopolis, the personal is political.

Various figures of the Establishment are mocked in this play. – such as the Persian Ambassador and his pretensions; such as the soldier Lamachus, who appears in full armour; such as Euripides, asked to provide rags for Dikaiopolis from his supposed cohort of beggars and cripples.

The central Greek city of Megara, which had access to the Corinthian and Saronic Gulfs, features largely in *The Acharnians*. Megara had a complex relationship with Athens. Athens sought to exclude Megara from the harbours and markets of its Empire – when, why, or exactly how, is unknown. But there is enough there for Aristophanes to treat the matter in comic mode. In keeping with comedy's stress on the body, this comes down to food and sex.

Megara, it is claimed, has no food, while the Theban can produce all sorts of food. As Brecht said, 'Food comes first, then morals'. But in an overwhelmingly agricultural world, this is very exaggerated. Three prostitutes, practitioners of oral sex, allegedly caused the Peloponnesian War. Athens stole one prostitute from Megara; Megara stole two from Athens. Such were the mouths that launched the Peloponnesian War.

The ending of *The Acharnians* finds Dikaiopolis enjoying the Anthesteria festival of the god Dionysus. The emphatic ritual of a sacred marriage mutates into Dikaiopolis appearing with two dancing girls, who hold his prick between them, while the very prominent drinking of wine sees Dikaiopolis drinking neat wine in one go (water was usually added to wine). The sterility of war yields to types of fertility.

The influential Athenian politician Kleon is savagely satirized in *The Knights* (424). Previously in 426, Kleon had accused Aristophanes' play *The Babylonians* of 'slandering the city in the presence of foreigners' at the City Dionysia. So much for the doctrine that poetry makes nothing happen.

Kleon had in 425 won a spectacular victory over the Spartans at Sphacteria in the southwest Peloponnese, bringing to Athens 300 hostages. This made Kleon extremely popular. He could dine at public expense in the Town Hall and, despite *The Knights*, he was elected one of the ten generals.

Kleon has always been controversial. Both Aristophanes and Thucydides brand him as a demagogue; for the historian, Kleon was 'the most drastic of citizens'. But Pericles, the leader without blemish, was of the same ilk. And both came from wealthy backgrounds. Recently there has been a strident attack on Kleon: 'revolting'; 'repellent'; 'appalling'; 'loathsome'; 'evil'. But in the 19th century, the radical English politician George Grote supported Kleon, idealizing him as 'a man of the opposition, whose province it was to supervise and censure official men for their public conduct'.

In *The Knights*, Kleon is burlesqued as a foreign slave from Asia Minor, the Paphlagonian. He terrorizes two other slaves, the Athenian generals Demosthenes and Nicias. The core issue in the play is the nature of politics, the extent to which the People (*Démos*) exercises power. The poorest citizen class in Athens came to over fifty per cent of the population, and was viewed as fickle by commentators like Aristophanes and Thucydides. In *The Knights*, the sausage seller engages in a contest with the Kleon character. They exchange abuse about bribery and the interpretations of oracles. The sausage seller provides an example of corruption: Demos refuses to spend money on warships, when it can spend money on pay for officials and jurymen.

In the end, the sausage-seller defeats Kleon, the Paphlagonian. The People (*Démos*) promises to reform.

The two most important generals in the early Peloponnesian War were killed in northern Greece in 422: the Athenian Kleon and the Spartan Brasidas. This paved the way for peace, so that the Peace of Nikias (to last 50 years) came into effect in 421. A few days before that, Aristophanes' play *Peace* was staged at the City Dionysia.

Peace employs one of Aristophanes' most fantastic conceits. *The Acharnians* and *The Knights* are mild by comparison. Trygaeus, an elderly wine grower from Athens, with no money, flies to the gods on a dung beetle. Such a creature exists, and eats shit; great play is made with this bizarre phenomenon, which reaches even Zeus, 'shitting enthroned in heaven'. A basic physical function that highlights human reliance on the body. This is later exploited by Swift to bring down to earth women: 'Celia shits'.

The gods, tired of the Greeks, have moved away from their abode to avoid war (they had no problem taking part in the Trojan War). There remains War, a ferocious monster, who threatens destruction of Prasice (in Attica), Megara, and Sicily. War throws Peace into a deep dark cave. Plato famously held that those confined to such a cave could have no grasp of reality. Eventually, the gigantic statue of Peace is rescued to the delight of Trygaeus.

Peace posits a radical binary opposition between peace that stresses what is festive and war that stresses what is malign. So the farmer's sickle contrasts with the soldier's weapons, spear, sword, shield. Trygaeus speaks of an 'end to war'. Celebration is clearly called for, with only the arms manufacturers losing out.

A rejuvenated Trygaeus, who has been without a woman for many years, marries Harvest (*Opóra*). They enjoy a magnificent banquet of food and drink: wine, hare, figs, cakes. The god of marriage Hymenaeus is invoked at length, with reference to the sex he presides over.

ARISTOPHANES, *THE CLOUDS*

This play was not a success when staged in 423; it came last in the competition. *The Clouds* was rewritten, but never performed. *The Clouds* mocks the intellectual revolution of the fifth century as put into effect by the group called the Sophists, and by Socrates, who becomes a character in the play. Old certainties about human life, about the gods, were now brought into question. While the Sophists were paid teachers, Socrates did not charge.

The Sophists specialized in Rhetoric, the art of speaking in public, as required in the Assembly, in the law courts. Their take on this was, allegedly, relativistic: they could make the weaker argument defeat the morally superior argument. In *The Clouds*, there is a contest between Right and Wrong, with Wrong asserting that there is no such thing as Justice (Plato's *Republic* is about the concept of Justice).

The leading Sophist was Protagoras (about 490-420). He famously maintained that 'Man is the measure of all things' (compare the Choral Ode on Man in Sophocles' *Antigone*). This assertion could suggest relativism and could also suggest atheism. But Protagoras is an agnostic: 'Concerning the gods, I am unable to know either that they exist or that they do not exist. For there are many obstacles: the obscurity of the matter and the brevity of human life' – while the character 'Socrates' in *The Clouds* asserts that the gods are no longer current (not the view of the historical Socrates).

Socrates wrote nothing, and preferred to ask questions rather than to promulgate doctrine. He concentrated on ethics, issues of right and wrong; seeing proper knowledge as the key to ethical decisions. If you know what is right, you will do what is right. But this, alas, ignores moral weakness. In Plato's early dialogues, Socrates seeks to define moral qualities: as Piety in the *Euthyphro*. But no definition is arrived at. There is a failure to get a result (*aporia*). Those questioned by Socrates might not be happy.

The Clouds takes place in the Thinkery (a comic version of what was to become the Academy of Plato, the Lyceum of Aristotle). The Thinkery is first frequented by a father named Strepsiades (Twister), then by his son Pheidippides. Strepsiades seeks to use the Thinkery to avoid paying debts, a radical distortion of what philosophy is about. But he is unable to learn. When Wrong wins the contest with Right, Pheidippides learns from this, and turns on his father. With the result that Strepsiades burns down the Thinkery.

This is very far from the celebration (*kómos*) that is usual in comedy. Far, too, from the fire of the Pre-Socratic philosopher Heraclitus, seen by him as the essential material of the world. Comedy can be dark.

ARISTOPHANES, *WEALTH*

This play of 388 signals the end of Old Comedy in Athens. *Wealth* is very short at 1209 lines; the role of the chorus and of the contest (*agón*) is seriously reduced; there is no *Parabasis*. For all that, *Wealth* is a play for our times since it stresses people's excessive desire for money. Noted, later, by Timothy: 'The root of all evils is the love of money.' Not money as such, but lust for money.

The god named *Wealth* is an old man who is blind (brought about by Zeus). Without discrimination, he rewards good men and bad men. So in order to ensure he acts properly, he must be cured. This occurs at the port of Athens, Piraeus, in the temple of the healing god, Asclepius. The poor man Chremylus is then enriched by Wealth, but things are not so simple: 'everything in the world is controlled by wealth' – an aphorism that predicts the nature of late Capitalism.

The horrific goddess Poverty is a vicious pest, who seeks to justify her role in the world. This she does by positing a sophistical distinction between living in poverty and living in penury. Allowing people to manage, to get by, makes poverty tolerable.

The absolute misery of penury is intolerable. Present day reality makes this distinction otiose: many in poverty do not cope.

Poverty can be sexual as well as material. A sexually frustrated old woman, who has resources, is dumped by her young man, when he gets money. Love, Eros is, like everything else, corrupted by wealth.

Still, Wealth is to be installed in the Athenian Treasury on the Acropolis. Robert Graves stated that there is no poetry in money; Aristophanes in *Wealth* proves otherwise.

ARISTOPHANES, *THE BIRDS*, *THE WASPS*

The Birds, a long play, was staged in 414 at the time of the Athenian expedition to Sicily. This massive enterprise, readily endorsed by the people of Athens, aimed to take control of the whole island of Sicily. This aim that did not take account of the size, the complexity, the resources of Sicily. Total disaster for Athens was to follow. A defeat in Syracuse in 413 involved the loss of 25,000 men and of 250 ships. Athens was never to regain its fifth century prominence.

The Birds posits a Utopia, an escapist fantasy that could suggest the idyllic expedition to the West, a Utopia that critiques contemporary life in Athens, and especially law suits. The law is the central issue of Aristophanes' play *The Wasps*: a satire on the jury courts in Athens. Positions as jurymen were much sought after, because male citizens over 30 were paid; and the numbers were very large – as seen in the trial of Socrates, (recounted in Plato's *Apology*). Comedy in *The Wasps* is centred on the clash between a father with a passion for jury service, and his son who attempts to stop this. In the black Utopia of Jack Cade's rebellion, the Butcher asserts: 'The first thing we do, let's kill all the lawyers.'

In *The Birds*, two men Euelpides (Good Hope) and Peisetairus (Friend Persuader) flee from Athens to a walled city in the air. The rulers there are personified birds, who have taken over from the gods. In Egypt, falcons and hawks were divine. This play sees the Chorus of 24 all costumed as different birds. An encyclopaedic aviary is to found a new city.

The immortal birds reign in Cuckoo in the Clouds – a place without ordinary social obligations, but one that offers health and long life. Unwelcome visitors from earth include Poets, Informers, Oracle mongers, Statute sellers.

Well established in this heaven, Peisetairus is to marry Sovereignty, a very beautiful woman, who manages the thunderbolts of Zeus. He proceeds to heaven, as the Chorus sing the wedding song to Hymen, god of marriage. An idyllic *kómos*.

The lyrics of *The Birds*, which require a musical setting, are justly renowned. As Yeats wrote, 'I found one poem that delighted me beyond all others; a fragment of some metrical translation from Aristophanes wherein the birds sing scorn upon mankind.'

6 – TWO TRAGEDIES DEALING WITH EVENTS IN HISTORY

AESCHYLUS, *THE PERSIANS*

This is the only extant Greek tragedy that stems from an event in history: the war between Greece and Persia (490-79), providing scope for the Greek obsession with opposites. Dating from 472, *The Persians* is also the earliest Greek tragedy we possess (Pericles was sponsor).

The scene is the Persian court of the capital Susa in the wake of the battle of Salamis in 480, in which a disciplined Athenian fleet defeated the Persians. This is vividly narrated to the court by a Messenger. Noting that the Persian fleet and army are gone, the Chorus of Old Men assert 'dead is the power of Persia'.

In *The Persians*, the focalization of both Athens and Persia is conducted by the Persians. A striking version of spin. The democratic collectivity of Athens is contrasted with the single ruler of Persia, Xerxes. A king given to arrogance (*hubris*), who must return to Susa in a defeated and pitiable state. A king punished by the gods.

What the writer Isocrates valued in Athens was *intellect*. Pater elaborates: Greek sculpture was 'a revelation in the sphere of art, of the temper which made the victories of Marathon and Salamis possible'. In Aeschylus, the Persian Queen Atossa learns about Athens from the Chorus. Athens has valiant soldiers, and its own wealth from the silver mines at Laurion.

The treatment of Persia in Aeschylus provides an early example of what the critic Said termed Orientalism: the mode in which Europe described the East, seen as a radical other. So

Persia is luxurious, emotional and dangerous. Difference is found even in personal names. For the Persians, there is over lexicalization, too many exotic names. For the Greeks, there is under lexicalization, no names at all. Another Eastern trait is the wearing of lavish clothes; the Greeks looked down on elaborate or gaudy dress.

The Persians deals with the material world, the world of war. But the play contains a strong non-material element. There is the punishment of the Persians by the gods. There is the Ghost of Darius, father of Xerxes, who refers to the further Persian defeat at the battle of Plataea in 479. There is the dream of Queen Atossa about the clash between Greece and Asia, symbolized by the two very elegant ladies, and the collapse of her son Xerxes.

The character 'Aeschylus' in Aristophanes' play *The Frogs* terms *The Persians* an 'excellent work'. A Persian view could be different. As in Robert Graves's poem 'The Persian Version': 'As for the Greek theatrical tradition' that views the Persian expedition 'as a grandiose, ill-starred attempt/To conquer Greece – they treat it with contempt'.

OCTAVIA

Octavia is the only play about Roman history that survives. Possibly written for the stage, but not by Seneca; it probably dates from the Flavian period (71-96). While non-Senecan in language and style, *Octavia* appropriates aspects of the tragedies of Seneca. It relates to the reign of Nero (54-68), and especially to the year 62, with the action being set in a three day period.

History here is not the general history of Rome, but the family history of Nero, last of the Julio-Claudian Emperors. The atmosphere is gloomy, claustrophobic, anti-imperial, suggesting that of the Gothic novel. Prose analogues in Rome are found in the historian Tacitus and the biographer Suetonius. To be specific: Seneca's theme of evil in the ruler (as in Atreus) is replicated in Nero. He is married to Octavia, daughter of the Emperor Claudius by his third wife Messalina. But Nero murders her (as well as his mother Agrippina), so that he can marry Poppaea Sabina in 58 – this despite popular rioting in favour of Octavia, who is supported by one of the two Choruses.

Octavia sees Nero as 'a savage tyrant' and Agrippina as a 'monster', one mirrored in the mythical and historical past: the murders of Iphigeneia; of Agrippina, whose Ghost appears; the rape of Lucretia. Nero sees power as an instrument to keep people in fear: 'let them hate, provided they fear'.

Just as in Seneca's tragedies there is a person who champions Reason, so in *Octavia* it is Seneca himself who tries to alleviate the excesses of Nero the megalomaniac. But to no avail. Nero is very deluded, claiming, without irony, that love is the chief reason for living.

Octavia paints a grim picture of Nero's reign. But this is not the whole picture. His first five years saw good government, honest administration, when Nero was guided by Seneca and by Burrus, who was in charge of the Emperor's bodyguard. Things did not go downhill until 58. Even after that, in 64 Nero provided relief for the fire in Rome. He can also be seen as a patron of the arts, including architecture. An exclusive obsession with the crimes of the Imperial family does not constitute history.

7 – EURIPIDES' LATE TRAGICOMEDIES

Euripides was ever the chameleon dramatist. A group of his late plays have the positive ending associated with comedy. These are tragicomedies that begin with an unsatisfactory situation and advance to a satisfactory conclusion. Plays that challenge the viewers' response. These late plays are *Helen, Ion, Iphigeneia among the Tauri, Orestes*. Similar in tone are the late 'romances' of Shakespeare: *Pericles, The Winter's Tale, Cymbeline, The Tempest*. Themes found in such plays are separation and reunion, marriage, recognition of children, the gods, escape.

Late Euripides paves the way for the comedy of Menander. As Wilde astutely saw, Euripides 'was to the age of Menander the model and the delight'.

EURIPIDES, *HELEN*

The myth of Helen provides a striking example of how different writers manipulate Greek mythology. What is central to *Helen* is the clash between appearance and reality. The traditional story of Helen has her brought to Troy by Paris from her husband Menelaus in Sparta. The Greeks try to get her back by fighting the Trojan War. But there is another story, already told by the poet Stesichorus in the first half of the sixth century. Now the Helen in Troy becomes a *phantom, the real* Helen lives in distant, exotic Egypt. So 'Not me, not in Troy, never set foot in it'.

The action of *Helen* in Egypt takes place seven years after the fall of Troy (there is much stress on the past). Egypt is ruled by king Theoclymenus (invented by Euripides), whose sister is the seer Theonoe. Much centres on the issue of identity: which woman is the real Helen? Can it be the *phantom* Helen? But she disappears. So the Egyptian Helen must be the *real* Helen, who is finally accepted by her shipwrecked husband Menelaus. This opacity of identity mirrors the opacity of language as expounded by the sophists and by Socrates. To know yourself, you must first know who you are.

The real Helen confronts a pressing problem: Theoclymenus wants to marry her, wants to kill any possible Greek rival. A method of escape for Helen and Menelaus must be found. Theonoe helps them arrange a spurious funeral at sea for Menelaus. The ship provided brings the couple to Greece. Helen is no longer beautiful and bad; she is now beautiful and good. But the Trojan War has been fought for the sake of an illusion.

The conclusion of the play is endorsed by the gods. Helen's deified brothers, Castor and Polydeuces, guide her and her husband home and ensure that Theoclymenus acquiesces in what has happened.

'Demonized, idolized, allegorized, or humanized. Helen is still here' (Blundell). Not just in the mythology and literature of the distant past. But also in the recent past: Yeats writes many love poems that see his beloved Maud Gonne as Helen of Troy.

EURIPIDES, *ION*

Recognition is the key to this tragicomedy. It concerns the young man Ion: who is he? Who are his parents? Aristotle held that recognition involving a person is the most effective type. Ion the protagonist will come to know what was previously hidden – the circumstances of his birth.

The action of *Ion* takes place in front of the temple of Apollo at Delphi, seen as the centre of the world. The god hides a sexual secret: he has fathered a male child by Creousa, a royal Athenian. She exposes the child, but he is brought by Hermes to Delphi to serve Apollo. Many mistakes now occur. The childless king of Athens, Xuthus, husband of Creousa, finds out that Ion is his son. He is not. Creousa believes that Ion is the illegitimate son of Xuthus, and tries to kill him. He is not.

Eventually, it emerges that Ion is the son of Apollo, and that Creousa is his mother. This double recognition brings about a reversal in the fortunes of Ion. In tragedy, in *King Oedipus*, Oedipus' recognition that he has killed his father and married his mother means that the reversal is ruin. But in *Ion*, recognition means the reversal is success: Ion will be king of Athens, and ancestor of the Ionian race.

The mechanism by which Creousa is reunited with her son is a basket containing items she deposited there: a blanket she wove as a girl; a necklace; an olive wreath – a motif that was to have a long history. In Wilde's comedy *The Importance of Being Earnest* (1895), Jack Worthing's birth is established by items in Miss Prism's handbag: injury caused by a bus; a stain on the lining; her initials. This unmasking constitutes a favourable reversal of his fortunes, so that Gwendolyn is now his.

In *Ion*, the new scenario is outlined by the goddess Athena (*dea ex machina*). Ion will be a famous ruler throughout Greek lands; he and his mother are content. The Chorus of Creousa's female slaves end this tragicomedy on a note of absolute optimism: 'In the end good men receive what they deserve, while the very nature of a bad man means he will never prosper'. Wilde's Miss Prism seems to agree: 'The good ended happily, and the bad unhappily. That is what Fiction means.'

EURIPIDES, *ORESTES*

Orestes is, arguably, the most radical of Euripides' plays. The original plot moves far beyond Aeschylus' *Oresteia*, Sophocles' *Electra*, even Euripides' own *Electra*. But for all that, the past of the Trojan War and of the House of Atreus weigh heavily upon the present – a present in which nearly every character is morally bad.

The first part of *Orestes* sees Orestes in a seriously disturbed state: his guilt at murdering his mother has made him mad. He is now to be judged not by the Court of the Areopagus in Athens, but by the public Assembly of the citizens of Argos, where widely divergent views about what to do with Orestes are heard (compare the Athenian Assembly). The herald Talthybius is a trimmer. Diomedes argues for banishment. Another man wants Orestes stoned to death; yet another man opposes this, and wants Orestes rewarded. But the majority voted for Orestes' death. He promises to commit suicide.

The tragic motif of Revenge then enters the play. When Helen's husband Menelaus refuses to help Orestes and Electra, they plan to kill Helen in revenge. But in due course Helen, self-interested, disappears. The pair then decide to kill the innocent Hermione. But the love theme of comedy is not far away. The scenes involving Orestes, his friend Pylades and Electra include expression of love, embraces, kisses, alerting us to the fact that *Orestes* is far from being an orthodox tragedy.

Eventually, impasse is reached. As when the foreign slave does not know what has happened to Helen; as when Orestes and Menelaus quarrel about the morality of killing women. The principle here is what Bakhtin terms the impossibility of any final solution (unfinalizability). Just as Ibsen's plays do not offer neat solutions. Divine intervention is required: the god Apollo as *deus ex machina*.

Most of Apollo's message concerns Orestes: he is to have a triumphant new life, as in comedy. In Athens, Orestes will be acquitted of matricide by the gods. He will marry Hermione, a central concept of comedy (as Pylades will marry Electra, and Menelaus a new wife). More: Orestes will rule in Argos, so that the personal and the political coalesce.

The final word about Orestes must go to the Chorus: 'here is a novelty succeeding novelties'.

EURIPIDES, *IPHIGENEIA AMONG THE TAURI*

Euripides is large, he contains multitudes. Aulis in central Greece in *Iphigeneia in Aulis* makes way for the exotic, barbarian Crimea in *Iphigeneia among the Tauri*. Both Iphigeneia and her brother Orestes experience a very different life in *Tauri* from that of other plays by Euripides, despite the stress on the past of the two central characters.

Iphigeneia is an 'articulate, expressive, brave and intelligent heroine' (Hall). She has metamorphosed from a sacrificial victim at Aulis to becoming a priestess of the goddess Artemis. But one who must preside over the sacrifice of Greek foreigners. This elevated position ensures that Iphigeneia is deprived of what is crucial for a Greek, a city (*polis*), together with the family and community that go with it. (Athens, says the goddess Athena, is 'a god-built city'). But the Taurian king Thoas is not impressed with Greek modes of behaviour: Orestes' murder of his mother would not be tolerated by a barbarian. Shipwrecked, Orestes (with Pylades) finds himself among the Tauri, and facing death.

Recognition is crucial to *Tauri*. Iphigeneia must find out who Orestes is; he must find out who she is. Though dreaming that Orestes is dead, Iphigeneia wants a letter brought to Argos re Aulis (anachronism). Orestes now knows who she is, and

Iphigeneia knows who he is because of his possession of Pelops' lance.

It is now imperative that Iphigeneia, Orestes and Pylades escape by sea, bringing with them the image of the goddess Artemis. Athena, *dea ex machina*, gives instructions to Orestes and Iphigeneia. He is to establish a temple of Artemis at Holae in Attica, where the priest will draw human blood to compensate for the last sacrifice of Orestes. Iphigeneia is to be in charge of the temple of Artemis at Brauron, also in Attica.

Tauri ends on a positive note. It shares the escape motif with *Helen*. It shares the motif of identification through material objects with *Ion*. It envisages a fine future for Orestes, not in politics as in *Orestes*, but in religion: the gods are served.

Still? Pound said, 'I would a temple to Artemis in Park Lane.'

EURIPIDES, *CYCLOPS*

Athens in the fifth century provides the dramatic genres of tragedy, comedy and tragicomedy. But the city also provides satyr plays that, at the City Dionysia, follow on from three tragedies by the same dramatist. Satyr plays present a burlesque treatment of Greek myth, and so belong to the comic spectrum. Greek tragedy can, on occasion, do comedy: as when Cadmus and Teiresias support the god Dionysus in the *Bacchae*. This is a phenomenon found also in Shakespeare: the Porter in *Macbeth*; the Gravediggers in *Hamlet*; the Fool in *King Lear*. But we do not know how a particular satyr play might relate to the preceding tragedies. Nor do we know about the psychological effects of satyr plays upon the audience.

Euripides' *Cyclops* is the only complete satyr play we possess. Even by the usual standards of Greek plays, it is very brief: 709 lines. Like a modern one-act drama? *Cyclops* derives from *Odyssey 9*, a work that itself anticipates the comedy of manners.

Cyclops posits a radical opposition between the barbaric Cyclops and the civilized Odysseus. The Cyclops Polyphemus has no city (*polis*): a loner, he rejects government. The matter of food and drink looms large in this play: the Cyclops eats lamb and cheese, he drinks milk. But this one-eyed monster is also a cannibal who eats men raw. An extreme example of a moral relativist, as the Sophists were thought to be. (Polyphemus in Theocritus II is very different, a lover of Galatea).

Odysseus is the antithesis of the Cyclops. He comes from the civilized island of Ithaca, as opposed to the barbaric Sicily of the play. He is clever, as Polyphemus is dumb. But above all, Odysseus is the owner of considerable quantities of wine, the drink sponsored by Dionysus, the drink consumed by civilized people. Prized more than wealth and available to all. Significant for the social institution of the symposium.

It is no accident that wine is the undoing of the Cyclops. Odysseus, who does not drink here, gets Polyphemus drunk on wine, then, with an olive stake, burns his one eye. Ensuring that the Cyclops is no longer in control of his cave and his captors there. There is a paradox here: symbols of civilization like wine and the olive are employed in order to execute a barbaric act. But one which is necessary.

Cyclops has the successful ending of comedy: Odysseus and the satyrs go home by boat to Ithaca, to civilization. These satyrs are far removed from characters in tragedy, being half animal; being selfish, unreliable, addicted to sex and to booze, and yet seeing fit, as they forget the past, to term themselves 'the model of modernity'.

W.D. Howells said 'What the American public always wants is a tragedy with a happy ending'. Lots of that in Euripides.

8 – MENANDER, PLAUTUS, TERENCE

Menander's dates are roughly 361-290. After the battle of Chaeronia in 348, Macedonia controlled the rest of Greece, including Athens. So by the time Menander came to write plays, the city of Athens was much reduced in stature. Comedies were no longer to be *public*, as in Aristophanes, and concerned with large issues such as war. Instead, comedy became *private*, depicting the ordinary life of bourgeois families – a type of play later espoused in Rome by Plautus and Terence.

The comedies of Menander, Plautus and Terence exhibit what Jakobsen terms the *dominant*: 'the focusing component of a work of art: it rules, determines, and transforms the remaining components'. For these comic dramatists, the dominant is the love of a young man for a young woman. Despite obstacles such as the blocking character of the man's father, this relationship comes to fruition: the pair get married – an example of social integration to be celebrated (*kómos*). Happy endings are desirable, even if not true.

This plot line is found in Menander's *The Bad Tempered Man*, in 14 out of 20 plays by Plautus, and in all 6 of Terence's comedies.

A variety of other stock characters frequent these comedies: cunning slaves; rapacious pimps; angry old men; boastful soldiers; women as either virgins or prostitutes – owing something to the character sketches of Theophrastus. Bergson asserts that 'Every comic character is a *type*', and is inflexible. But the comedies of Menander, Plautus or Terence manipulate, constantly, cleverly, their stock characters.

But are these comedies 'funny'? The plays of Menander and Terence fail to arouse exuberant laughter, more quiet contemplation of the incongruous. Plautus is different, very. His plays can be wonderfully funny, not least when depicting the machinations of the clever slave (they owe something to the Atellan farces of Campania).

In 1900, Menander hardly existed as text. But in 1905, substantial parts of 5 plays were discovered. Then in 1957 came the only complete comedy of Menander that we possess. Entitled *The Bad Tempered Man*, this play of 316 is apprentice work. A notable example of which is that it includes half a dozen characters *without names* in a striking instance of under-lexicalization. So the rich young man Sostratos falls in love, while hunting, with *The Girl*. As though to validate Marlowe: 'who ever loved that loved not at first sight?' The matter may not be so simple. It could be that Sostratos is in love with love. His hanger-on Chaereas thinks so: 'Was that your idea when you came out, to fall for a girl?'

Knemon, a poor farmer, the girl's father, is the play's blocking character; a bad tempered man who is against the world. Sostratos tries to impress Knemon by going down to his level, by working in the fields. To no avail. When Knemon falls down a well, he is rescued by his stepson Gorgias – suggesting the death and resurrection of the god of Theatre, Dionysus.

Intricate family relationships now develop. After Knemon makes Gorgias the guardian of his daughter, Gorgias entrusts her to Sostratos, whose father Kallipides gives his daughter to Gorgias. Engagements like this require the formula used by the father of the groom in Athens: 'I give you this woman for the ploughing of legitimate children.' In *Antony and Cleopatra*, Agrippa notes of the son of Julius Caesar and Cleopatra: 'He ploughed her and she cropped.'

Marriage in *The Bad Tempered Man* is not smooth. Knemon is reluctant to integrate into society, to take part in the dancing. In any case, the marriages do not take place today, but tomorrow, outside the play.

Menander had an indifferent, if lengthy, career as a dramatist, winning just 8 prizes. But his apotheosis lay in the future, mediated through Plautus and Terence. Segal points out that 'Menander is arguably the single most important figure in the history of Western comedy'. Witness Machiavelli (*The

Mandrake); Shakespeare (*The Comedy of Errors*); Molière (*The Miser*); Wilde (*The Importance of Being Earnest*).

The theme of incest features in plays by Menander. Incest in Greek thought meant sexual relations between two persons in the same family: parent and child, brother and sister. This violation of the natural order was deemed to be an abomination. The paradigm in Greek literature is Oedipus, the son who married his mother.

Menander brings the theme of incest down to the day-to-day world, explored among the mundane life of ordinary people. In *The Shorn Hair*, the young man Moschion falls in love with the young woman next door, Glycera (Sweetie). His passion is ardent. But this would be an incestuous relationship, since Glycera is his sister. This fact is eventually discovered, which leads Glycera to marry someone else, the soldier Polemon (War) who had been already involved with her (a second marriage also occurs).

At the time Polemon believed there was a relationship between Moschion and Glycera, he cut her hair. In the 7th and 6th centuries, Greek women wore their hair long. But in the Hellenistic era of Menander, young women wore their hair in a variety of ways. These included allowing a little hair over the forehead, and having hair in a ponytail. Pope notes the significance of female hair when cut in 'The Rape of the Lock'.

The Samian Woman is typical of Menander: a young man named Moschion rapes a young woman named Plangon, and makes her pregnant. But Moschion is suspected, by his adopted father, of seducing his father's mistress, a courtesan from Samos called Chrysis (Goldie). A relationship that has the potential for incest.

Nikeratos castigates Moschion by citing tragedy (as characters in Menander often do). Notorious perpetrators of incest are Oedipus and Thyestes who seduced his own daughter. Moschion is even worse than them. Eventually, the numerous errors of the play are resolved, so that Moschion marries Plangon.

These two comedies play with the theme of incest, but it is avoided. As always in New Comedy, what is sexually permissible is socially endorsed marriage.

Reception Studies usually deal with the way Greek and Roman material is used in later eras, right up to the present time. But Reception could also exist in ancient Rome, when Latin authors appropriated material from earlier Greek authors. This particular instance of Reception is virtually unknown in antiquity. For comedy, what is involved is how Plautus and Terence engage with the plays of Menander and others.

Eliot describes this type of literary appropriation: 'Immature poets imitate; mature poets steal; bad poets deface what they take, and good poets make it into something better, or at least different'. This gives the lie to Cicero's assertion that early Roman tragedies are 'Latin short plays taken word for word from Greek ones', for the comedies of Plautus and Terence *manipulate* their Greek predecessors, as is made clear by comparing part of Plautus' play *Bacchides* with a long fragment of Menander's *Double Deceiver* (discovered in 1968). Plautus combines two separate speeches in the original; he changes the rhythm from iambic to trochaic; he adds exuberant jokes; he attacks the Roman ethical concept of *pietas*, loyalty to country, family, friends. Plautus steals.

(We could not know that before a good deal of Menander became available. Ignoring Plautus' originality, people tried to recuperate the Greek text by translating the Latin, word for word, into Greek verse à la Menander, as Wilde did with part of *The Pot of Gold* by Plautus).

Roman comedy introduces material that is specifically Roman: the worship of the god Bacchus; bribery at elections; the ceremony of the triumph; the punishment of slaves.

Laughter in Rome extended to many aspects of life. From the Romans, we may have 'learnt how to laugh and what to laugh *at*'. (Beard). Rome had the concept of a repertoire of jokes, as in the collection called *Laughter Lover*. We observe this in the character named Galasimus (Mr Laughter) in Plautus' comedy *Stichus*. This man is a *parasite* who flatters people in order to get a free lunch or dinner, and who tells them jokes. Galasimus owns private joke books, and boasts that 'I'm selling jokes ... you won't find better jokes anywhere'.

Laughter can be scripted in Roman comedy. In Terence's play *The Eunuch*, the parasite Gnatho, eager to please the boastful soldier Thraso, bursts out laughing: '*hahaha*'. This over the top reaction is a response to an old joke of Thraso. But it is clear that the verbal expression mimics human laughter.

Plautus often elicits laughter – lots of it – in situations akin to farce; in language that achieves sophisticated humour. This holiday atmosphere is a far cry from strict codes of behaviour that were officially espoused in Rome. Plautus doesn't do decorum. By comparison, Terence is low key, claiming to write a 'quiet' type of play, which may explain why his comedy *The Mother in Law* failed on two occasions; rope dancing and a boxing match won out in 165; a combat of gladiators in 160.

Plautus and Terence differ in several other ways. More than 60 songs adorn the comedies of Plautus (not the case in Greek New Comedy). Usually introduced with the entrance of one or more persons on stage, the songs stress emotions like sorrow, joy, fear, so that Plautine comedy is a kind of musical. Hence Sondheim's version of Plautus: *A Funny Thing Happened on the Way to the Forum* (1962). But Terence has hardly any lyrical songs.

Plautus and Terence differ in their use of the Prologue. But both dramatists employ the Prologue in order to gain the favour of the audience.

In *The Rope* of Plautus, the Prologue expounds the essential elements of the plot. In his *Pseudolus*, the Prologue is meta-theatrical: 'a long play by Plautus is coming on stage'.

An aesthetic programme is outlined in the Prologues of Terence. Later Latin writers like Catullus and Horace did the same. Part of Terence's strategy is to attack his dramatic rival Luscius Lanuvinus, who advocated close adherence to the original Greek comedies. This raises the question of *contaminatio* (blending together): can a Roman comic dramatist such as Terence appropriate in a single work, not just one Greek play, but *two*? Terence opts for two. *So his Woman of Andros* adapts not just Menander's comedy of the same title, but also his further comedy *The Woman of Perinthus*. This is another instance of how Roman comic drama is not slavish in its use of Greek material.

Plautus does not seek to purify the dialect of the tribe. His use of Latin, his idiolect, is brilliantly exuberant – Latin involving hyperbole; colloquial terms of abuse; military terms; triplicate phrases; Greek words Latinized; puns; diminutives. Terence's Latin, on the other hand, does seek to purify the dialect of the tribe. Indeed he is described by Julius Caesar as 'a lover of pure language' (*puri sermonis amator*).

Aphorisms feature in the comedies of Menander, Plautus and Terence. They state some general principle in a highly condensed form that is often paradoxical. Menander gives us: 'The male whom the gods love dies young.' This is taken up by Plautus as 'The male whom the gods love dies a young man.' Byron notes the antiquity of this aphorism: '"Whom the gods love dies young", was said of yore.'

Terence can be taken in an aphorism to assert a universal truth. *The Eunuch* gives us: 'Nothing is now said that has not been said before.' *The Woman of Andros* gives us: 'The quarrels of lovers are the renewal of love.' But an aphorism of Terence may be more mundane: 'I am a human being: I think nothing human foreign to me.' This is spoken by a nosey man intent on prying into his neighbour's business.

Wilde is one of the great masters of aphorisms that can be counter cultural: 'Work is the curse of the drinking classes'; 'A cynic is a man who knows the price of everything and the value of nothing.'

The character of the slave is crucial to Roman comedy. These slaves are of varying type, trustworthy and unscrupulous, serious and witty. One outstanding type is the trickster, an irreverent being who contrives to bypass social boundaries. This involves lies and deception (in real life, slaves were usually reliable). This scenario ensures *levelling* between master and slave, although in the end hierarchy is restored. Compare Bertie Wooster and Jeeves in Wodehouse: 'His hapless dependence on Jeeves is funny partly because the servant ought not to be superior to the master' (Orwell). In such Plautine comedies, the role of the cunning slave is to assist the young man of the household to win the young woman by means of ingenious schemes.

Plautus' comedy *The Ghost Story* is a striking example both of the clever slave in action, and of the boy-meets-girl theme. It is a masterpiece. The young man Philolaches is in love with a young woman Philematium, a music girl. He buys her with borrowed money; frees her; installs her in the house of his father, who has been away for three years.

There is in this comedy a strong stress on sexual love and on enjoyment – in short, on pleasure. Philolaches asserts that 'Love soaked right through my heart'; while Philematium's slave Scapha indulges in bawdy talk. The house puts on a non-stop party, with girls, drinks, singing; and the inevitable drunk in the form of Callidomates (contrast the puritanical slave from the country, Grumio). But there is a very pure note: the beauty of Philematium, enhanced by clothes, powder, rouge.

The clever slave Tranio becomes in his element on the sudden return of the father. Philolaches exclaims, 'I'm dead, Tranio, we're both destroyed.' But Tranio will solve the problem by a pack of lies, by deceiving the master. To prevent the master entering his house, he pretends it is haunted by the ghost of a murdered man (Rome liked ghost stories).

The reviled money lender now appears, wanting his interest on the loan to Philolaches. Tranio informs his master that it was used to buy the house off the neighbour next door, Simo. Simo allows the father to inspect his house. But the truth must emerge, Tranio is exposed, to be punished by whipping torture or death (power that, in real life, masters exercised over slaves).

Tranio takes refuge at an altar, making him untouchable. But in comedy there must be a satisfactory ending. Callidomates, friend of Philolaches, persuades the father, at some length, to forgive both his son and the slave Tranio.

Terence's comedy *The Woman of Andros* (his first in 160) explores the intricacies of love: 'Love gilds the scene, and women guide the plot' (Sheridan). In Terence that involves a *double* plot, one that deals with several women; one that culminates in two marriages (*As You Like It* ends with four). This manipulation of the boy-meets-girl theme is matched by manipulation of the cunning slave theme: Davos is not at all a successful trickster.

Simo wants his son Pamphilus to marry Philumena, the daughter of his friend Chremes. But this man, though previously a model, has seduced Glycerium, the sister of a woman named Chrysis, who came from the island of Andros (the most northerly of the Cyclades Islands in the Aegean). Chrysis is poor and isolated, so that she becomes a courtesan. It is striking that when she dies in this comedy, her funeral is stressed.

Sorrow, too, arises from the love of Pamphilus and Glycerium: *hinc illae lacrimae* in the famous tag, 'from this situation come those tears'. (Terence has 24 instances of tears). Meaning here that Simo withdraws his consent to the marriage of Pamphilus.

This impasse calls for the cunning slave Davos, but he is out of his depth, even though Simo brings himself to say, 'I think you're to be trusted'. Davos first persuades Simo to go ahead with the wedding in the hope that Pamphilus will end his affair with Glycerium. But this wedding is turned into an on-off matter, becomes, as it were, a theatrical prop. Complicated further by the fact that Glycera has a baby.

To cut a long story short, Glycera is found to be a freeborn Athenian, so that Pamphilus can marry her, she is in fact Chremes' daughter. He provides her with a very large dowry (one of the largest in Roman comedy).

THE BRAGGART SOLDIER

This comedy of Plautus portrays a soldier who boasts about his achievements to an extraordinary degree (this type appears in 6 other Plautine plays). Thraso in Terence's *Eunuch* does not *boast*, but is witty. To boast is the comic equivalent of tragic arrogance (*hubris*). So the opening scene of this play sees the soldier Pyrgopolynices boasting of how he overcame 7,000 men in a single day. But the slave Palaestrio tells the audience 'He's so full of crap and lechery, no lies are vaster'. Falstaff plays many roles, but they include the braggart soldier. This seasoned campaigner boasters 'I am a rogue if I were not at half-sword with dozens of them in two hours together'. Even the boasting of Pozzo in *Waiting for Godot*, can be linked to Plautus.

Plautus' soldier has campaigned in exotic lands in the Greek East; he mentions the Seleucid king of Syria. His play is very clear about soldiers returning to Rome – as from the Second Punic War in 201-201 – men who might be part of Plautus' audience.

Here the boastful soldier is a lover, as though to invert Ovid's assertion that every lover is a soldier. Pyrgopolynices is a rival of Pleusicles for the woman Philocomasium. The soldier uses violence by forcing her to go with him to Ephesus in the Greek East.

The conclusion of *The Braggart Soldier* is striking. Pleusicles and his beloved escape by ship to Athens (compare Euripides' *Helen*). This is the usual happy ending. But what happens to the braggart soldier is far from usual. The cook Cario threatens him with castration, and demands from him an enormous sum of money to be let go. The soldier accepts he has been tricked, and acknowledges he is being punished for lechery. More: the moral is, the soldier says, 'There would be less lechery if lechers were to learn from all this.' They would abandon lust. A very new take for Plautus on men in love.

THE ROPE

This comedy of Plautus is a source of great pleasure, with an engaging plot and characters, a very original work. It will have advanced on a Greek comedy by Diphilus. The setting of *The Rope* is remarkable. The street setting in Athens is abandoned. Instead, the action takes place on the rocky coast of Cyrene in Eastern Libya, a Greek foundation. Reference is made in *The Rope* to that city's staple export of the plant silphium, used as a luxury food with pungent flavour, and as a drug for medical conditions.

The Rope deals with the usual love interest. The young man Plesidippus, son of Daemones, loves Palaestra. But she is owned by a pimp named Labrax, viewed by others as utter scum. When in his possession, Palaestra and her friend Ampelisca are shipwrecked, and end up in Cyrene. They take refuge in the Temple of Venus. But the love story plays a very minor role in *The Rope*.

Most of *The Rope* is taken up with an intricate series of vivid exchanges between the characters and have little to do with the love theme. Noteworthy are a set of different Slaves, together with their masters. Sceparnio, far from knowing his place, is seriously truculent. Trachalio is in pursuit of the pimp Labrax. Gripus has grandiose ideas: he fancies himself as an entrepreneur and claims to have founded the city of Gripolis. Pathos occurs in the exchange between Palaestra and Ampelisca.

Commentary on *The Rope* is offered by the divine Arcturus and by Daemones. Speaking the Prologue, Arcturus, who spies on the action, knows that bad people like Labrax will be punished. Daemones dreams that an ape steals swallows from their nest. Labrax?

Gripus the fisherman brings about the conclusion of *The Rope* – as a *homo ex machina*, a man, not a god, from the machine. He obtains from the sea a strange catch in the form of a trunk. Gripus engages in a contest with Trachalio for possession. Eventually, the trinkets in the trunk – a tiny silver sickle, a gold locket – turn out to belong to Palaestra, who is found to be Daemones' daughter. So Plesidippus is free to marry her. And Tracchalio, freed, is to marry Ampelisca. Gripus gets a lot of money from Labrax who, in the end, is invited back to society. All's well that ends well.

But this is a comedy. When Daemones lectures Gripus in a moralizing speech, Gripus replies in a meta-theatrical way: 'I've heard actors in comedies spouting that sort of stuff.' The play's the thing.

THE PRISONERS

Lessing, believing that comedy should have an ethical purpose, called *The Prisoners* 'the best comedy ever put on the stage'. Hyperbole. To which Norwood offers a very different appraisal: 'crass nonsense'; 'gulf of ineptitude'. What cannot be contradicted is that *The Prisoners* is unlike other plays by Plautus: this comedy is unique. Being, for a start, serious in tone, as seen in the striking loyalty of the slave Tyndarus to his master Philocrates; he risks his life to free his master from captivity. Then *The Prisoners* has no women characters, with the result that the usual boy-meets-girl theme is absent. This point is stressed by the Prologue and Epilogue (possibly post-Plautine). There is to be no rehash of old ideas, no love affairs, no stock characters like a pimp, a braggart soldier.

Where, then, is the comic element in *The Prisoners*? Most obviously in the parasite Ergasilus, dependent on Philopolemus. As befits his type, this man is obsessed with going on about food to a ludicrous degree. All that matters is that he has an empty stomach. And his jokes that are designed to flatter no longer work. But in the end, Ergasilus is satisfied, since he can enjoy the best of food, and, by exchanging roles, wants to organize a banquet, which is often the mode of celebration in comedy.

Clever deception, in which characters swap identities and new identities come into being, provides a further comic element in *The Prisoners* (this deception is found in 7 other Roman comedies). The play ends when identities are sorted out – but not in relation to boy-meets-girl. In order to recover Hegio's captive son Philopolus, the slave Tyndarus and his master Philocrates exchange places, exchange roles. When this trick is discovered, Hegio sends Tyndarus to the dire punishment of the stone quarries. Eventually, Hegio gets back his two sons: Philopolemus, and the once stolen Tyndarus, now recognized as Hegio's son.

Critics who read *The Prisoners* can object to discrepancies involving *time*: how can the activities of Ergasilus fit into the conventional one-day limit? The answer is that, on the stage, this and other discrepancies will be of no significance.

CODA

1

Shakespeare's early play *Titus Andronicus* shows his fellow dramatist Marlowe how things should be done: with scorching rhetoric, with endless horrific violence. The Shakespearean scholar Kenneth Muir asserts re *Titus Andronicus* that it 'is a nice irony that Shakespeare's most shocking play should be closest in spirit to the classics'. *Titus* includes two quotations in Latin from Seneca's tragedy *Phaedra*, and a cannibal meal from Seneca's tragedy *Thyestes*. There is no irony here, nice or otherwise. Greek tragedy is not conservative, tame, full of decorum. The plays are riddled with violence and sex. People faint at a performance of *Titus*.

2

George Steiner wrote a book called *The Death of Tragedy* (1996); Erich Segal wrote a book called *The Death of Comedy* (2001). They are praisers of the past, including the Greco-Roman past. But Greek plays from the fifth century continue to resonate today. The dramatist Frank McGuinness, who has made versions of four Greek plays, notes that it 'seems to be happening through the English-speaking world, that the Greeks are emerging as the dominant international force in our theatre'. This is the case, above all, in Ireland, with some 40 versions of Greek plays by leading poets and dramatists. In this at least, we are all Greeks.

WORKS CITED

Arkins, B., *Builders of My Soul: Greek and Roman Themes in Yeats* (Gerrards Cross 1990).

---, *Irish Appropriation of Greek Tragedy* (Dublin 2010).

---, 'The Theme of Opposites: Yeats and Oedipus' in: *European Voices in the Poetry of W. B. Yeats and Geoffrey Hill*, eds. I. Bochting, J. Kilgore-Caradec, E. Muller (Bern 2015), 45-53.

Arnold, Matthew, *Poems*, ed. K. Allott (Harmondsworth 1954).

Bartel H, & Simon, A., *Unbinding Medea* (London 2010).

Beard, M., *Laughter in Ancient Rome* (Berkeley 2014).

Bevis, M., *Comedy – A Very Short Introduction* (Oxford 2013).

Blondell, R., *Helen of Troy* (Oxford 2013).

Boyle, A.J., *Tragic Seneca* (London 1997).

---, *Roman Tragedy* (London 2006).

---, *Seneca, Oedipus* (Oxford 2012).

Bradbury, M. & McFarlane, J., eds., *Modernism* (Harmondsworth 1985).

Burkert, W., *Greek Religion* (Oxford 2004).

Churchill, Caryl, *Seneca, Thyestes* (London 1995).

Cline, E.H., *The Trojan War* (Oxford 2013).

Davies, J.K., *Democracy and Classical Greece* (Fontana 1978).

De Jong, I.J.F., *Narratology and Classics* (Oxford 2014).

Dillon, J. & Wilmer, S., *Rebel Women* (London 2005).

Drakakis, J. & Liebler, N.C., eds., *Tragedy* (London 1998).

Duckworth, G.E., *The Nature of Roman Comedy* (Princeton 1952; London 1994).

Easterling, P., ed., *The Cambridge Companion to Greek Tragedy* (Cambridge 1997).

Egan, Desmond, *The Death of Metaphor* (Gerrards Cross 1990).

Eliot, T.S., *The Sacred Wood* (London 1967).

---, *The Poems*, eds., C. Ricks & J. McCue (London 2015).

Feeney, D., *Beyond Greek* (Cambridge, Mass. 2016).

Finley, M.I., 'The Athenian Empire' in his *Economy and Society in Ancient Greece* (Harmondsworth 1983).

Foley, H., Foley, quoted in Halperin (1990).

---, 'The "Female Intruder" Reconsidered: Women in Aristophanes' *Lysistrata* and *Ecclesiazusae*', *Classical Philology* 77 (1982), 1-21.

---, *Female Acts in Greek Tragedy* (Princeton 2001).

Fraenkel, E., *Plautine Elements in Plautus* (Oxford 2007).

Fraud, S., *Jokes and their Relation to the Unconscious*, Standard Edition, Vol. 8, ed. J. Strachey (London 2001).

Goldhill, S., 'The Audience of Athenian Tragedy', in *Easterling* (1997), 54-68.

---, *Aeschylus, Oresteia* (Cambridge 2004).

Graves, Robert, *Poems* (Harmondsworth 1961).

Hall, E., *Inventing the Barbarian: Greek Self-Definition Through Tragedy* (Oxford 1989).

---, Introduction to *Euripides, Bacchae and other Plays*, trans. J. Morwood (Oxford 1999).

---, Introduction to *Euripides, Heracles and other Plays*, trans. R. Waterfield (Oxford 2003).

Halperin, D., *One Hundred Years of Homosexuality* (New York 1990).

Hanson, J.A., 'The Glorious Military' in *Roman Drama*, eds. T.A. Dorey & D. R. Dudley (London 1965), 51-85.

Hardwick, L., *Reception Studies* (Oxford 2003).

Harrison, Tony, *Dramatic Verse 1973-1985* (Newcastle-Upon-Tyne 1985).

Hawthorn, G., *Thucydides on Politics* (Cambridge 2014).

Hine, H.M., *Seneca, Medea* (Warminister 2000).

Hunter, R.L., *The New Comedy of Greece and Rome* (Cambridge 1985).

Jenkyns, R., *The Victorians and Ancient Greece* (Oxford 1981).

---, ed., *The Legacy of Rome* (Oxford 1992).

Joyce, James, *Stephen Hero* (London 1981).

Kavanagh, Patrick, *Collected Poems* (London 1973).

Kemp, P., ed., *The Oxford Dictionary of Literary Quotations* (Oxford 1999).

Kennelly, Brendan, *When Then is Now – Three Greek Tragedies* (Northumberland 2006).

Kerrigan, J., *Revenge Tragedy: Aeschylus to Armageddon* (Oxford 1996).

Kott, J., *Shakespeare Our Contemporary* (London 1965).

Lloyd–Jones, H., *Sophocles, Antigone, Trachiniae, Philoctetes, Oedipus at Colonus* (Cambridge, Mass. 2002).

Lodge, D., ed., *Modern Criticism and Theory* (London 1993).

Macintosh, F., *Dying Acts* (Cork 1994).

MacNeice, Louis, *The Poetry of W.B. Yeats* (London 1979).

McGuinness, Frank, quoted in *Amid Our Troubles*, eds. M. McDonald and J.M. Walton (London 2002), 280.

Muir, K., *The Sources of Shakespeare's Plays* (London 1977).

Orwell, George, *Essays* (London 2000).

Pater, Walter, *Greek Studies* (London 1925).

Poole, A., *Tragedy – A Very Short Introduction* (Oxford 2005).

Pound, Ezra, *Sophocles, Women of Trachis* (London 1969).

---, *Selected Prose 1909-1965* (London 1973).

Richards, I., *Principles of Literary Criticism* (London 1967).

Ross, I., *Oscar Wilde and Ancient Greece* (Cambridge 2013).

Said, E., *Orientalism* (London 1978).

Schopenhauer, A., *The World as Will and Representation* (New York 1969).

Seaford, R., *Euripides, Cyclops* (Oxford 1984).

Segal, E., *The Death of Comedy* (Cambridge, Mass. 2001).

Segal R.A., *Myth – A Very Short Introduction* (Oxford 2004).

Selden, R., *A Reader's Guide to Contemporary Literary Theory* (Brighton 1985).

Shaw, M., 'The Female Intruder: Women in fifth century Drama', *Classical Philology* 70 (1975), 255–66.

Silk, M., & Stern, J., *Nietzsche on Tragedy* (Cambridge 1981).

---, *Aristophanes and the Definition of Comedy* (Oxford 2000).

---, et al, eds., *The Classical Tradition* (Oxford 2014).

Steiner, G., *Antigones* (Oxford 1984).

---, *The Death of Tragedy* (New Haven 1996).

---, *After Babel* (Oxford 1998).

Stevens, Wallace, *Opus Posthumous*, ed. S.F. Morse (London 1959).

Stoppard, Tom, *Rosenkrantz and Guildenstern Are Dead* (London 1967).

Sullivan, J.P., ed. *Ezra Pound* (Harmondsworth 1980).

Vernant, J.-P. & Vidal-Naquet, P., *Myth and Tragedy in Ancient Greece* (New York 1990).

Walsh, D., *Literature and Knowledge* (Middleton 1969).

Wells, C., *The Roman Empire* (Fontana 1984).

Winnington-Ingram, R., *Euripides and Dionysus* (London 1997).

Woolf, Virginia, *A Room of One's Own* (Flamingo edition).

---, 'On Sophocles' Electra' in *Sophocles, Critical Essays*, ed. T. Woodard (Englewood Cliffs, N.J. 1996).

Worth, K., 'Greek Notes in Samuel Beckett's Theatre Art' in *Dionysus Since 69*, ed. E. Hall et al. (Oxford 2005), 265-83.

Yeats, W.B., *The Variorum Edition of the Plays of W.B. Yeats*, ed. R.K. Alspach (London 1966).

---, *Autobiographies* (London 1980).

---, *A Vision*, 1925 version, eds C.E. Paul & M.M. Harper (New York 2008).

REFERENCES

1 Poole (2005); Bevis (2013).
1 Easterling (1997); Silk (2000); Hunter (1985).
1 Silk & Stern (1981).
1 Goldhill in Easterling (1997), 54-68.
1 *Don Juan*, Canto III, ix.
1 Stoppard (1967), 23.
1 Richards, (1967), 194.
2 Schopenhauer (1969), 1; 254
2 Kavanagh (1973), xiv.
2 Segal (2004).
2 Stevens, (1959), 178.
4 Aristotle, *Poetics* 13; Steiner (1998), 477.
4 Quoted in Kemp (1997), 126.12.
4 Pound: T.S. Eliot in Sullivan (1970), 67-80.
5 Eliot (1967).
5 Quoted in Jenkyns (1992), 266.
5 *A Vision* (1925), 204.
5 Arnold, quoted in Jenkyns (1981) 105.
7 Bakhtin, quoted in Lodge (1993), 138.
9 Shaw (1975), 255-66; Foley (1982), 1-21; Dillon & Wilmer (2005).
9 *A Room of One's Own* (Flamingo edition), 49.
9 In Halparin (1990), 208.
10 Bartel & Simon (2010).
10 *Dramatic Verse 1973-1985* (Newcastle-upon-Tyne 1985), 371.
10 Kerrigan (1996).
10 W. Congreve, *The Mourning Bride* 3.8.
11 Hine (2000), 14-15.
11 Preface to *Poems* (1954), 262.

11 Steiner (1984).
11 Macintosh (1994).
12 Sophocles (2002), 28.
14 Winnington-Ingram (1997).
16 Dillon (2005), 222-33.
17 Segal (2004), 87-90.
17 Arkins (1990), 125-26.
17 Kemp (1999), 45.2.
20 Arkins (2015), 45-53.
21 Boyle (2012).
22 Arkins (1990), 136-38.
22 Burkert (2004), 203.
23 *The Spanish Tragedy* (1592), 4.1.97.
23 Egan (1990), 121.
23 *Essays* (2000), 359.
23 Vernant & Vidal-Naquet (1990), 161-79.
24 de Jong (2014).
25 Nemeans 3.22.
26 Kott (1965), 35.
26 *Macbeth* 5.3.22-26.
28 Pound (1969), 22; 71; 66. Pound (1986), 796.
28 Hall (2003), xxvii.
29 Nashe: Arkins (2012), 52.
29 *The Spanish Tragedy*, 1.3.48.
31 Churchill (1995), vii.
31 Cline (2013).
33 Finley (1983), 161.
35 Arkins (2009), 99.
35 Jenkyns (1981), 91.
35 Goldhill (2004).
38 Woolf (1966), 122.
39 *Stephen Hero* (1981), 173.
42 Bradbury (1985), 99.
42 Eliot (2015), 113-27.
42 Walsh (1969), 136.
43 Davies (1978), 139.
43 Preface to *Poems* (1963).
44 *The Threepenny Opera*.
45 Thucydides 1.36; Jenkyns (1980), 80.
46 'The Lady's Dressing-Room'.
48 Graves in Kemp (1999), 147.4.

49 *Henry VI, Part Two*, 4.2.71.
49 *Autobiographies* (1980), 171.
51 Hall (1989).
51 *Greek Studies* (1925), 260.
51 *Orientalism* (London 1978).
52 *Poems* (1961), 162.
53 Wells (1984), 126-32.
55 Ross (2013), 176.
55 Blundell (2013).
56 Blundell (2013), 249.
58 Hall (1999), xviii-ix.
59 Pound (1973), 53.
59 Seaford (1984).
60 Kemp (1999), 63.7.
61 Selden (1985), 14-16.
62 *Hero and Leander.*
62 Segal (2001), 154.
63 Hardwick (2003); Silk et al (2014).
64 Feeney (2016).
64 Eliot (1967), 125.
64 *De Finibus* 1.2.4.
64 Segal (2001), 187; Fraenkel (2007).
64 Ross (2013), 211-3.
64 Beard (2014), 212.
64 Beard (2014), 8-14.
64 Orwell (1994), 295.
68 *The Rivals.*
68 Hanson (1965).
68 Worth (2005), 278.
70 Duckworth (1967), 152.
72 Muir (1977), 23.
72 McGuinness (2002), 280.